The Jewish Town of Prague

by

Arno Pařík
Pavel Štecha

OSWALD

Text © Arno Pařík
Photographs © Pavel Štecha
   © Dana Cabanová (pp. 20, 30, 42, 48, 54,
   60, 72, 78)
   © Roman Maleček (pp. 38)
   © Archív Židovského muzea v Praze
Translation © Gita Zbavitelová
   © Dušan Zbavitel
Design © Bohumil Karas
Editor Helena Osvaldová
Published by OSWALD ©, Jankovcova 21, Praha 7,
Phone 876280
1st Edition 1992
Printed in Czechoslovakia by GRAFIATISK Děčín
ISBN 80-85433-16-8

2

The statue of Moses on his knees at a moment of despair over the fragments of shattered tablets of the Law after his descent from Mount Sinai was made by Czech symbolist sculptor František Bílek at the turn of the century. The statue was meant to be the first of an unfinished series of numerous Biblical characters and prophets to demonstrate the spiritual development of mankind. The statue was placed in a small park in front of the Altneuschul in 1935 but was destroyed by the Nazis during World War Two. A new copy was unveiled in the same place in 1948.

Prague is one of the oldest and most important Jewish centres in Central Europe. Due to Prague's position in the middle of the country, its Jewish community became a natural administrative centre for the other Jewish communities in Bohemia, which is why its history constitutes an essential part of the history of Jews in the whole kingdom. Despite countless natural catastrophes, pogroms and attempts at expulsion in the thousand-year-long history of the Jewish community of Prague, there has never been a disruption of the continuity of the local Jewish settlement and religious life. On the contrary, Prague's Jewish Town became, in various historical periods, an asylum for many co-believers expelled from adjacent countries and also temporarily one of the most populated Jewish communities in Europe.

The illuminator of the richly decorated Bible of Václav IV from around 1400 presented Biblical scenes and characters in contemporary clothes and typical pointed Jewish hats, most probably the way the Prague Jews looked in the 14th century.

The oldest Jewish settlement in Prague

The participation of Jewish merchants in Prague's markets in the early Middle Ages is described in a report by the Arab-Jewish merchant Ibrahim ibn Jacob in 965. In those times, the Jewish community was probably settled around the Count's market-place near Hradčany Castle. In the late 11th century, King Vratislav moved his royal residence to Vyšehrad Castle in whose vicinity another Jewish settlement in Prague was recorded in 1091. The existence of the Jewish community in the village of Malá Strana (Lesser Town) near Hradčany Castle, however, is documented again in the early 12th century. Apart from these Jewish settlements near the two castles in Prague, another Jewish community was founded, most likely in the late 12th century at the latest, near an international marketplace on the right bank of the Vltava river, along the road connecting the oldest fords in Prague, on the territory of what was to become the Jewish Town.

Reports on the changing position of the oldest Jewish settlements on the territory of Prague testify to the considerably free status of Jews in society. They enjoyed the same rights as groups of Romance and German merchants in Prague with the same privileges granted by the Count. They were free to settle along trading routes or near marketplaces, to trade and engage in crafts, and their communities were fully autonomous. The Jews in Bohemia most likely dealt in natural products such as furs, grain, wool, fabrics, tin and wax but also, in cattle, horses and slaves. They imported exotic commodities such as expensive textiles, jewels, weapons, salt, wine and oriental spices. Because of their education, they also worked as physicians or office clerks, e.g. Jacob Apella in the court of Vladislav I.

Prague's early mediaeval Jewish community not only flourished economically but also was an important cultural centre. Prague's oldest preserved Hebrew manuscript is the 12th century commentary of a Talmudic treatise by Isaac ben

Jacob called Laban. His pupil Abraham ben Azriel was head of Prague's community and is well-known in Hebrew literature as the author of an analysis of the synagogal liturgy "Arugat ha-Bosem" (A Patch of Balsam) from the early 13th century. It seems that Chladek's pupil was Isaac ben Moses (ca. 1180—ca.1250) , also called Isaac Or Zarua according to his main work, who studied in Talmudic schools in Northern France and came back to Prague after spending many years in Jewish communities in the Rhineland. His comprehensive work "Or Zaru'a" (Scattered Light), a commentary of Talmudic ritual laws, was quoted and imitated in Germany, Poland and Italy. His son's abbreviated version became popular among Jews all over Europe. To explain difficult Hebrew terms in their manuscripts, Abraham ben Azriel and Isaac Or Zarua use many old Czech words and names, demonstrating their excellent knowledge of the Czech that the Jews living in Premyslide Bohemia used as their everyday language.

Prague's Ghetto
in the Middle Ages

The first change in the originally free position of the Jews in mediaeval society resulted from the first Crusade in 1096—99 which was accompanied by pogroms also in Prague in 1096. When the Prague Jews were just about to move out of the country for fear of repeated persecutions, Count Břetislav II had their property confiscated. The legal status of the Jews, however, deteriorated considerably under Pope Innocent III as a result of the verdict enacted by the Fourth Lateran Council in 1215 which prohibited Jews from owning land and engaging in agriculture and trade, and limited their economic activities basically to money lending and pawnbroking which were forbidden for Christians to practise as usury. The Council's subsequent decisions called for minimum contacts between Jewish and Christian inhabitants, their settlement in separate districts and compulsory distinctive Jewish dress or identification.

These religious decrees resulted in the end in the almost total economic and social segregation of the Jews from the other inhabitants, thus contributing to the creation of anti-Jewish superstitions, e.g. that the Jews desecrated the host and performed ritual murders, which became a cause of numerous bloody pogroms in the High and late Middle Ages, and even later on. Stripped of their rights and outcast to the very fringe of society, the Jews became dependent on the caprice of rulers who proclaimed them as their property and direct subjects. To obtain a permit to settle in the country which was just a temporary and often formal promise to provide the basic legal protection, the Jews now had to pay high regular and, if necessary, also special taxes to the ruler, often providing the most reliable source of his income.

The 13th century is an important turning point in the development of Prague and its Jewish community. Under King Wenceslas I the settlements scattered on the right bank of the Vltava river became a town whose fortifications also surrounded the newly established settlement of St. Gallen as well as the Count's older marketplace near the Old Town Square, settlements of foreign merchants and the Jewish community at its northwestern end. At that time we can already distinguish some main concentrated areas of the Jewish settlement on its territory. The oldest seems to be the settlement near the Old Synagogue (Altschul) which has always been an independent community and was separated from the Jewish Town during all its history. The other part of the mediaeval ghetto was the settlement alongside its main road called then "Inter Judaeos" (Among the Jews) which was subsequently named Dlouhá, Josefovská and Široká street. This road was wider in its middle part, forming a sort of longitudinal square where the business life of the ghetto and its public festivals took place from the old times to the last century. In the north the youngest part of the mediaeval ghetto came to exist in the proximity of the Altneuschul which was built in the last third of the 13th century. The Altneuschul testified to the distinguished position of Prague Jewry and has always been its spiritual centre. It has never been surrounded by neighbouring houses like the majority of the ghetto's other synagogues and outside its eastern facade a sort of small square appeared, emphasizing the synagogue's prominent position. With more and more houses in the neighbourhood, the whole area of the mediaeval ghetto was enclosed in a wall and the entrance to the ghetto was barred from the Christian districts with six gates to protect the Jews who, according to new privileges, became the property and servants of the royal chamber. Although the ghetto formed a kind of enclosed enclave in the Old Town as early as in the Middle Ages, on its borders there was always property owned by both sides. In the Golden Lane behind the ghetto's gate, for example, the house of Lazarus the Jew was situated, which was, after his death, donated by Charles IV to the University of Prague, but returned into Jewish hands after 1386.

Frequent persecution for religious reasons on the one hand, and the rulers' increasing need of financial means on the other, called for the necessity of readjusting the legal status of the Jews in the mid-13th century. In the beginning, special privileges were granted by Friedrich II to the Austrian Jews in 1244, then Pope Innocent IV issued a Bull to protect the Jews in 1247, and finally Bela IV granted privileges to the Hungarian Jews in 1251. Inspired by the abovementioned decrees, King Přemysl Ottokar II also adjusted the legal status of the Jews in the Czech lands on March 29, 1254. The privileges specified the status of the Jews as direct subjects of the King who guaranteed his protection and allowed them to deal in money and engage in money lending and pawnbroking. The privileges prohibited violence against the Jews and their property, proclaimed the superstition that the Jews used human blood for ritual purposes was untrue, and forbade violent baptism, disturbance of Jewish festivals and desecration of and causing damage to cemeteries and synagogues. Violence against the Jews was to be regarded as damage to the royal property and therefore subject to severe punishment. Jewish communities were promised the freedom to practise their religion, considerable independence in their internal affairs, and permitted to establish their own administration and courts. A royal "Jewish judge" was appointed to deal with disputes between Jews and Christians.

Přemysl Ottokar II's privileges legalised the position of Jews in the Czech countries for a long time and were reconfirmed by his successors in principle. Nevertheless, some events in the period that followed show what the royal protection looked like in practice. Václav II who succeeded Přemysl Ottokar arrested Prague's and rural Jews and released them only after they paid a high ransom. Similarly, John of Luxembourg arrested representatives of Prague's Jewish community in 1336 and seized synagogal property by force. Václav IV, too, arrested the representatives of Bohemian Jewish communities in 1385 and confiscated their possessions.

In the 14th century anti-Jewish riots broke out, particularly in Germany, affecting also Bohemia. The biggest mediaeval pogrom, however, took place in Prague in 1389, at Easter which was observed on the last days of the Jewish festival Passover that year. As a consequence of the alleged consecration of host and religious intolerance instigated by priests in Prague's churches, a large mob of Prague's citizens attacked the ghetto on April 18, and overwhelmed it. The angry mob ransacked, looted and burned Jewish houses where many victims were burned alive. Even those who sought refuge in the Old Synagogue and Altneuschul did not escape violent death. Blood could be noticed on the walls of the Altneuschul for centuries. The pogrom cost some 3,000 lives of ghetto inhabitants including children, women and old men whose corpses were burned en masse in the streets even on the days that followed the pogrom. One of the few who survived the catastrophe was Prague's rabbi-to-be and poet Avigdor Kara (d. 1439) who wrote a dirge which is recited on Yom Kippur at the Altneuschul every year to this day.

The position of Jews as direct royal subjects did not last too long. The ruler lost control over Jewish affairs as a result of the Hussite wars that consequently weakened the influence of the Catholic Church and royal power in favour of the nobility and independent towns. Catholics regarded Hussites as a judaising sect while they, indeed, and among them especially radical Taborites, identified with Biblical Israel. The Jews sympathised with the Hussites in their struggle against the Catholic Church and particularly German crusaders, and helped them, among other things, build fortifications at Vyšehrad Castle in 1420, or supported them with money. The contemporary rabbinical authorities also expressed their sympathy for the Hussites and it is generally believed that it was Prague's Rabbi Avigdor Kara who to some extent influenced the very Hussite movement which seemed to fulfil the messianic hopes of Judaism. The Hussite revolution reduced feudal social relations making it possible for the Jews to acquire some professional skills at least to a limited extent. Some Hussite theologians also found the main cause of the Jews' inferior position in society in the forced reduction of their economic activities to money business, and recommended that they should also be given a chance to engage in agriculture and trade. Despite Jewish sympathy for the Hussites, however, anti-Jewish pogroms broke out, e.g. in Prague in 1422.

The greater independence of towns whose inhabitants increasingly dealt with trade and finance resulted in the expulsion of Jews from many towns in Germany, Austria and Silesia as a consequence of growing competition and in 1454 the Jews were also driven out of all the royal towns in Moravia. The period of weak reign of Vladislav of Jagellon was marked by repeated disputes among the ruler, noblemen and towns about the control over Jewish affairs. Many Jews were still controlled by noblemen or towns but they often had to pay to both town councillors and noblemen as well as to the king.

In Prague, the entire political and judicial powers of the royal Jewish court as well as the authority to levy Jewish taxes had been usurped by the Old Town administration during the Hussite wars. It is probably due to these circumstances that Prague's Jewish community escaped severe persecutions in the 15th century. At the Landtag in 1501, Vladislav of Jagellon took the Jews into his protection, promising that they might remain in Prague and the Czech lands if they paid 500 three-scores of silver as an annual tax for the royal protection. Although the Jews of Prague also contributed to the town treasury, the Old Town burghers insisted repeatedly in 1502, 1507 and 1509 that the Jews be expelled from the town as well as from the whole country. But the King refused by issuing the Olomouc Edict in 1510 reconfirming the old privileges of the Jewish community.

Renaissance in the Jewish Town

With the accession of Ferdinand I to the throne in 1526, the Czech countries became part of the Hapsburg domains. It seemed that central royal power would be strengthened, also improving the still uncertain position of the Jews. In his efforts to regain control over Jewish affairs, Ferdinand I fell out with the Czech Estates as well as with burghers who repeatedly asked for the expulsion of Jews. Frequent slander accusing the Jews of smuggling silver out of the country or acting as spies in the war with Turks, and the accusation that the Jews affected the establishment of judaising sects in Bohemia, finally made Ferdinand I decide to drive them out of both Prague and the whole kingdom in 1541. The Emperor postponed the deadline for the expulsion twice but in 1543 most Jews had to move out of Prague. Only those rich enough to buy a decree of protection, and several families taking care of the remaining communal affairs, were allowed to stay in Prague on special permits. The expulsion was temporarily lifted with another decree only in 1545. In 1551, instigated by the Old Town burghers, Ferdinand ordered the Jews to wear a distinctive humiliating earmark in the form of a yellow circle. Another expulsion from Prague and the whole country followed in 1557 at the request of Archduke Ferdinand, Bohemia's Vice-Regent. Again, the deadline for their withdrawal was postponed by supplications and intercessions, again protection decrees were granted to individuals, again the outcasts were robbed and mugged on the road. A year's postponement was granted to Prague's Jews by Maximilian II on the occasion of his coronation in 1562 but the expulsion was called off only in 1563.

Despite the unsafe position of Prague Jews in the first half of the 16th century, the Renaissance entered the Jewish Town as early as the beginning of the century, through the establishment of the first Hebrew printing house in Central Europe. At first it was managed by a group of printers among whom a predominant position was gradually achieved by Gershom ben Shalomo ha-Kohen and his sons. After 1527 they were granted the privilege of being the only printers of Hebrew books in Prague, by King Ferdinand I. Among Prague's oldest Hebrew prints excelling in typographic layout and decoration, the Book of Benedictions from 1514 should be mentioned as well as editions of the Pentateuch from 1518 and 1530, and particularly the so-called Prague Haggadah dating from 1526 which is generally considered to be one of the most beautiful early Hebrew prints. The best-known member of the large Gersonide family was Mordecai ben Gershom who, assisted by his five sons, printed the most significant Prague Hebrew prints of the 16th century, e.g. writings by Rabbi Loew and David Gans.

The most prominent sponsor of the oldest Hebrew prints was Isaiah Halevi Horowitz (d. 1519) whose son Aharon Meshullam Horowitz (d. 1545), after the expulsion in 1541, helped at least some of the ghetto's inhabitants to stay in Prague through his protector Lev of Rožmitál, Prague's burgrave. The Horowitz family was one of the most influential families in Prague's ghetto. They played the role of court bankers, possessing various privileges. The prestigious position of the family at the dawn of the Renaissance is also reflected in the fact that they had their own private (now Pinkas) synagogue, a big building with a rich late-Gothic and Renaissance decoration which was completed in 1535.

After the death of Ferdinand I, a long period of misery and uncertainty was replaced with one of great economic and cultural prosperity for Prague's Jews. Maximilian II reconfirmed Jewish privileges in 1567 and issued a decree lifting the ban for Jews to engage in trade. In 1571 the Emperor, his wife Maria and courtiers visited Prague's Jewish town and received the Rabbi's blessing.

Rudolph II ascended to the Bohemian throne in 1576 and moved his residence to Prague where the eccentric but tolerant and art-loving Emperor soon concentrated a colourful international company of diplomats, prominent scientists and artists as well as astrologers and alchemists in his court. In 1576 Rudolph II reconfirmed the privileges granted to the Jewish community by his predecessor, assuring the Jews that they would not be expelled from Prague now or in the future. Rudolph II resolved the dispute with the Old Town burghers by confirming the allegiance of the Jews to the Emperor's jurisdiction and also in the years 1593 and 1602 the Emperor again protected the Jewish community from the Old Town guilds. In 1599 he exempted it from all taxes and tolls in Prague's towns. Under Rudolph II, the Prague Jewry regained its former independence and the development of trade, finance and crafts brought about the unprecedented relaxation of life in the ghetto, where the number of inhabitants increased considerably. King Matthias, too, treated Prague's Jewish community with favour, reconfirming all its privileges and former prerogatives in 1611.

During the Renaissance, individual personalities, prominent thinkers and artists as well as wealthy bankers and patrons of the ghetto loomed large in community life. The most prominent figure in the Renaissance ghetto was Mordecai Maisel (1528—1601), court Jew and financier to Rudolph II. His name is linked with the majority of structures built in Prague's Jewish ghetto, whose development as well as future layout were now completed. Maisel's family had been settled in Prague for generations. In 1576 he became a member of the Board of Jewish Elders and later achieved the community's leading post. Probably towards the end of the 1560s, he took part in the construction of the High Synagogue and the Jewish Town Hall situated at the corner opposite the Altneuschul in the center of the Jewish Town, becoming a symbol of the ghetto's autonomy and independence. By buying new land, Maisel enlarged the area of the Old Jewish Cemetery and built a Talmudic school, a synagogue and a bath at its north-eastern edge. In 1592, he took advantage of a privilege granted by the Emperor himself and built at the southern border of the ghetto a synagogue of his own whose beauty, as his contemporaries testify, exceeded that of all the other buildings in the ghetto of those days. Mordecai Maisel was also a generous patron of the community's various charity organisations. He built a house of the Prague Funeral Society founded by Rabbi Eliezer Ashkenazi in 1564, supported several schools, a hospital and a poorhouse, and financed the paving of all the streets in the ghetto. He promoted the economic prosperity of the ghetto by lending money to craftsmen and the poor without interest, and gave great presents to other Jewish communities.

The dominating representative of Prague Jewry's spiritual life, however, was Maisel's contemporary Judah ben Bezalel called Rabbi Loew (1512—1609), known in Hebrew sources as MAHARAL. He was active in Prague from 1573 as rector of the local Talmudic school which became widely known under his leadership. In the 18th-19th centuries, the great personality of Rabbi Loew became the subject of folk tales and legends glorifying him as the creator of an artificial human being, the Golem, that considerably enriched, in various versions, the number of Prague Jewish legends. In fact, however, Rabbi Loew made his name immortal by his untiring pedagogic and organisational activities and as the author of ethical writings based on mysticism. His pupil was the mathematician, astronomer and first modern Jewish chronicler David Gans (1541—1613). In his historical book entitled "Zemach David" (Offspring of David), he recorded contemporary events of Prague's ghetto. Gans also wrote a book on astronomy "Nehmat ve-Na'im" (The Pleasant and the Agreeable) and kept in touch with Tycho de Brahe and Johannes Kepler, the prominent scholars in Rudolph's court. However, the most outstanding of Rabbi Loew's pupils was Yom Tov Lipmann Heller (1576—1654) who acted as Prague's Chief Rabbi; it is here that he wrote his important commentary on the Mishnah, which has become part of most editions of the Talmud since then.

The Ghetto in the Baroque period

As soon as the Czech Estates revolted in 1618, the town's poor assaulted the Jewish Town. A year later the Old Town burghers requested again that the Jews be expelled. Understandably under the circumstances, the Jews did not join the revolt. After the Battle of the White Mountain on November 8, 1620, the Jews were spared the persecution of the Emperor's troops but they had to undertake to provide a considerable loan for Ferdinand II's war expenditure and, before long, to agree to pay increased regular taxation.

At that time, the leading representative of Prague's Jewish community was the court Jew and financier Jacob Bassevi of Treuenburg (1580—1634), of Italian origin, who was the first Jew in the Hapsburg domains to be raised to the peerage. Owing to his assistance and friendly contacts with Vice-Regent Karl of Liechtenstein, the Prague Jewry managed to acquire 39 houses beyond the existing ghetto boundaries, despite the protests of the Old Town burghers, expanding the ghetto as never before. Since the Emperor could not do without the financial support provided by the Jews during the war, he reconfirmed all their former privileges in 1623 and 1627, including the freedom to trade and sell their own products in marketplaces throughout the country, the exemption from taxation and tolls in

Prague's towns, and a greater power of the Jewish Elders and Emperor's Jewish judge at the cost of the rights of the Municipal Court. Nevertheless, the ever-increasing taxes and extra payments imposed by the Diets in 1638 , a plague epidemic in the Jewish Town in 1639 and disruption of trade as a consequence of the war, nearly ruined the Jews. In 1648, the Jews took an efficient part in defending the Old Town against the Swedes and in recognition of their bravery, Ferdinand III granted the right to the Jewish community to use a Swedish cap in the middle of the Star of David as its emblem.

The hardship of the Thirty Years War and heavy taxation resulted in a considerable decrease in the number of the Jewish Town inhabitants. Despite this, the population of the Prague ghetto increased again with an influx of refugees from Poland and the Western Ukraine who escaped Cossack-led pogroms during the Chmielnicki uprising in 1648—49. The war with the Turks in 1663—64, too, resulted in another tax increase as well as a new wave of refugees from Hungary and Poland. When the Jews were expelled from Vienna in 1670, a large number of fugitives moved to Prague and other Bohemian and Moravian towns and villages.

The program which was supposed to limit the increasing numbers of the Jewry in Bohemia was prevented by a plague that claimed the lives of some 3,500 Prague ghetto inhabitants in 1680. Another disaster was a big fire which broke out on June 21,1689, in the Old Town, destroying all of the 318 ghetto houses and 11 synagogues and costing the lives of many ghetto inhabitants. After the fire the authorities attempted to limit the size of the Jewish Town and also considered moving the Prague Jewry to the quarter of Libeň or Štvanice Island. But thanks to financial assistance provided by Jewish communities abroad, the ghetto was quickly restored to its original size. Shortly after the fire in 1694, Prague's Jewish community was shocked by a controversial trial of the alleged murderers of the twelve-year-old convert Shimon Abeles, a culmination of the long-time Jesuit efforts to Christianise the Prague Jews.

Despite the abovementioned misfortunes and catastrophes that cost the lives of many, the number of Prague's Jews grew from about 6,000 at the start of the 17th century to 11,500 in the late 17th century, making it probably the largest Jew-

ish community in Europe, after Amsterdam and Salonica. Under Charles IV, the authorities continued to attempt to reduce the Jewish population in Prague and the Czech lands. To achieve this goal, the first census of inhabitants of all the Jewish communities in the country was taken in 1724 recording 8,541 Jewish families in Bohemia and 5,106 in Moravia. These figures also became a quota permitted to exist in the future. To keep the status quo, the so-called Familial Decree issued in 1724 stipulated that only the oldest son of the family could marry. Many of the second-born sons had to move out to Poland or Western Hungary if they wanted to get married. The decree considerably slowed down the demographic development of Jewry in the Czech lands for more than 120 years.

The census of the Prague Jewish Town's population was taken only in 1729, listing 2,335 Jewish families with 10,507 individual members. Out of 2,335 registered money-making persons in the ghetto, over 700 were craftsmen — mostly tailors, shoemakers, hat-makers, goldsmiths and butchers, but also barbers, bathkeepers and musicians.

The Silesian wars which broke out after the accession of Maria Theresa to the throne had tragic consequences for Prague's Jewish community. As a punishment for allegedly supporting the Prussian army during the occupation of Prague in September 1744, the Empress ordered the expulsion of Jews from Prague and Bohemia with the decree of December 18, 1744, while the Jews of Moravia and Silesia were expelled on January 2, 1745. Despite intercessions by the Bohemian vice-regency, court office and Estates as well as protests by the English, Dutch and Turkish ambassadors, Maria Theresa did not change her mind but only delayed the deadline for the Jews to leave Prague. On March 31, 1745, all the Jews except for the seriously sick had to leave and resettle at least two days' journey from the town.

The expulsion from Prague was reconfirmed in the spring of 1746 but the deadline to leave the country was extended by up to six years. In Prague the absence of Jews began to be apparent in business and trade which had neither market nor raw materials for production and consequently prices went up and taxation down. In September 1747, a hearing was given to representatives of all Prague's guilds, the majority of whom complained they had been damaged by the loss of

Jewish customers and suppliers. Their arguments finally made Maria Theresa give the Jews a temporary permit of residence in the Czech lands for the next ten years on July 14, 1748, while in August she let them return to Prague. At the same time, however, she imposed on the Jewish community a new, so-far highest „toleration tax" of 204,000 guldens a year which was increased every five years. The high taxation and yet another devastating fire in the Jewish Town in 1754 that destroyed 190 houses and 6 synagogues led to enormous debts being incurred by Prague's Jewish community which has never regained its economic importance.

Enlightenment and Emancipation

Almost until the end of the 18th century, the Jewish communities lived as totally independent administrative and social units with the traditional religious and language culture which basically did not change for centuries. Only the period of Enlightenment instituted considerable changes in the existing structure of the whole society. The development of trade, new forms of production and legal and social reforms began to create conditions also for a wider involvement of the Jews in the economic and cultural life of the society. The Josephine reforms brought about not only the formal equalisation of Judaism with other religions but also the abolition of special distinction of the Jews, permitting them to engage in trade, crafts and agriculture to an unlimited extent and encouraging them particularly to establish factories. The most significant changes for Jewry, however, were reforms in the field of education which made it possible for Jewish students to attend all sorts of private institutions of higher education and encouraged them to set up their own Jewish schools to instruct students in the German language, mathematics, geography and morality. With the government trying to introduce the German language in all administrative fields, an edict was issued instructing the Jews to keep their communal and business records in German, and another edict in 1787 stipulated that every Jew should adopt a German name. The Josephine reforms, however, abolished neither the Familial Decree nor the restriction concerning the place of residence and special Jewish taxation.

By the mid-19th century, the traditional Rabbinical education still kept up in Prague, the main representatives being Ezekiel Landau (1713—1793), the Chief Rabbi of Prague and author of the generally recognised collection of Halachic Responsa entitled "Noda bi-Yehudah" (It is Known in Judea), and his pupil Eleazar Fleckeles (1754—1826)) who was active as a member of the Rabbinical Collegium of Prague and as a preacher. Towards the end of the 18th century, however, Prague also became a centre of the new spiritual trend of Jewish enlightenment called Haskalah. The pioneers of radical enlightenment reforms in Prague included Herz Homberg (1749—1841) who promoted the establishment of modern Jewish schools and wrote a textbook of morality for them, entitled "B'nei Zion" (Sons of Zion), and Peter Beer (1758—1839), author of the first textbook of a history of Israel for Jewish schools. A moderate trend of Jewish enlightenment was represented by the brothers Baruch (1762—1813) and Judah (1773—1838) Jeiteles, Hebrew poets and contributors to the first periodicals written in Hebrew. An outstanding representative of this trend in Prague was also Shalomo Judah Leib Rapoport (1790—1867), Prague's Chief Rabbi from 1840 who edited a number of biographies of important personalities from the Jewish past. He was one of the pioneers of modern Hebrew. Editions of enlightenment literature were concentrated in the printing house of Moshe Israel Landau (1788—1844) who published, apart from fundamental writings of Judaism, also mediaeval Jewish literature and works by contemporary authors. The new Jewish intelligentsia was coming to the fore also in medicine, law and the humanities at the University of Prague. Favourable conditions for entrepreneurs were taken advantage of by the newly formed class of Jewish businessmen and industrialists. Prague's Jews asserted themselves especially in the textile industry. The largest factories of this branch were those of Porges Brothers from Portheim, Przibram Brothers, L. Epstein and L. Dormitzer. Other influential factory owners included Shimon and Leopold Lämmel, Moses and Leopold Jeruzalem, Moritz Zdekauer, Shimon Neustädtel and Israel Hoenig of Hoenisberg, who was a leaseholder of the Austrian tobacco monopoly and an army supplier.

Although the ghetto ceased to be an impenetrably separated enclave of the Old Town, its living conditions in the late 18th and early 19th centuries were gradually deteriorating. Except for a few patrician houses, the buildings in the ghetto were detrimental to health, overcrowded and insufficiently equipped in terms of sanitation. In the first half of the 19th century, a number of houses were rebuilt but the suffocating conditions of the ghetto did not offer much possibility or scope for considerable improvement of living conditions. In addition, more lots were used for building, flats were divided into smaller rooms and superstructures were built atop houses which made the streets look narrower and the light in them dimmer.

It is therefore not surprising that from the late 18th century wealthy individuals at least were trying to escape from the overcrowded Jewish Town. By 1806, they had acquired 89 houses in the immediate vicinity of the ghetto in Kaprová and Dušní streets, and at Jánský Square. This enlarged area was called "Under the Line" because it was separated from the Old Town with a wire marking out the area where the Jews were allowed to walk on Saturdays. In 1811 the Jews succeeded in obtaining another 28 houses in the area surrounding the Holy Spirit Church, and one year later, another enlarged area "Under the New Line" was established with further 53 houses by 1836. To buy houses in the Old Town outside the ghetto's territory was a privilege granted only to wealthy Jews who could show money of their own but the transaction involved many problems and was often prohibited without reason. As late as in 1846, Prague's Town Council tried to make the Jews move out of the houses and return to the ghetto.

The equality of the Jews with the other inhabitants was recognised only by the first Austrian Constitution in 1848. A year later, the forced residence in ghettos as well as the Familial Decree were abolished and the equality of Jews with Christians was affirmed under the law. In 1852, the Jews were granted the right to acquire houses and in 1859 the government confirmed the right of Jews to own land, tearing down the last barriers to their free economic activity. The Constitution of 1867 finally proclaimed full civic and political emancipation for the Jews of the Austro-Hungarian monarchy.

The incorporation of the ghetto in the union of Prague towns became an issue for consideration in 1849 but the project was implemented only in 1861 when the Jewish Town was proclaimed the fifth district of Prague. To commemorate the Josephine reforms and the Emperor's visit to the ghetto, Prague V was given the name Josefov. At that time, large numbers of well-off Jews started to move to better quarters in the neighbourhood of the Old Town Square, such as Celetná, Železná, Melantrichova and Na příkopě streets, the New Town and the newly forming quarter of Vinohrady.

The new parts of the Jewish Town were built mostly in the first decade of the 20th century. The rows of tenement houses abound in rich decoration in various historical styles and decorative elements from all times. We can find allegoric characters of the ancient past, busts of Bohemia's rulers and saints as well as Hussite fighters or Three Musketeers. We can also see the most varied heraldic coats-of-arms, patriotic slogans and excerpts from old chorals, but also inspired genii reminiscent of the figures painted in the posters by Alfons Mucha.

The reconstruction of the Jewish Town

With the withdrawal of wealthy inhabitants from the ghetto, Josefov changed into a quarter of Prague's poor regardless religion. The old buildings of the Jewish Town, which their original dwellers tried to keep in a usable shape were neglected and deteriorating quickly. The main reasons why Prague's town councillors decided to reconstruct the former Jewish Town thoroughly were overpopulation, high morbidity and mortality of its inhabitants, the danger of epidemics caused by insufficient sewerage, frequent floods and especially the complex problems of ownership which made it impossible to repair local buildings.

The town councillors had considered reconstructing the Jewish ghetto since it was connected with Prague's historical towns. The legal basis for the reconstruction was set by approving the law on indivisibility of house property in 1874 and the expropriation law in 1891. As early as 1882 the town council put up a contest for the best reconstruction project; the winner was designer Alfred Hurtig whose project with further adjustments was approved in 1889. It provided a basis

for the proper sanitation law which was passed in February 1893, and included all of Josefov with adjacent parts of the Old Town (as far as Platnéřská and Dlouhá streets), and the quarters of St. Adalbert and Podskalí in the New Town. In 1895 the town council's sanitation commission began to buy out real estate extensively, and two years later the demolition of the central part of the former ghetto started.

The building project called for a considerable elevation of the terrain's level to prevent floods. It also equipped the quarter with a modern system of sewers, a drinking water supply and new thoroughfares. The house-owners aimed to change the labyrinth of narrow lanes into a modern city quarter connected by way of Pařížská street with the Old Town Square at one end, and at the other the promenade on the river bank where the commercial and social life of the growing city could be transferred. The construction of new houses began around 1900 and most of the former Jewish Town was built within the following decade. The housing project became an example of Prague's architecture of the early 20th century. It

For centuries, the Altneuschul and High Synagogue along with the Jewish Town Hall have formed the very centre and spiritual axis of Prague's Jewish Town. These three buildings dating from the 13th, 16th and 18th centuries respectively, seem to recall the most significant periods of life of the mediaeval, Renaissance and Baroque ghetto. During the reconstruction, houses and streets in the vicinity of the synagogue disappeared; this was the end of the Dřevěný plácek (Wooden Square), V kolnách, Šmilesova and Poštovská streets, the Baroque house of the Moscheles family as well as the Great Court Synagogue with old butchers' shops and all of the northern part of Rabínská street. The former labyrinth of narrow lanes was replaced by Pařížská street situated high above the level of the former terrain where the Altneuschul seemed to sink deep. Proud facades of opulent tenement houses, a controversial memorial of the modern time, overshadow the last traces of one of the once most famous Jewish communities in Europe.

14

was conspicuous with spectacular decoration, plenty of gables, oriel windows and turrets, aiming to evoke a historical atmosphere but, in the first place, to meet the house-owners' demands for presentability.

The Jews themselves did not resist the sanitation reconstruction of the former ghetto which had been a symbol of inequality to them for centuries, and actually supported it. But before it started, representatives of the Czech cultural elite — such as writers Vilém Mrštík, Ignát Hermann, Zikmund Winter, and societies such as the Club for Old Prague, Umělecká Beseda (Artistical Society) or the Association of Engineers and Architects — protested against an inconsiderate reconstruction of the historical organism of the Jewish Town. Their protests grew stronger during the sanitation reconstruction, resulting in not only an increased interest of the public and artists in the preservation and documentation of the Ghetto's monuments but in adjustments of the project in at least some cases.

Since then the new housing in place of the former Jewish Town has become an oft criticised example of the insensitive approach to historical monuments and a lack of understanding of town-planning principles. Prague's Ghetto had had some 300 houses, thirty-one streets, several tiny squares and a lot of passageways and corridors interconnecting houses and yards. Today the same groundplan is divided into only ten streets with 83 tenement houses which are considerably higher than the former ones, forming impassable blocks.

In place of Prague's ghetto, a thoroughly new quarter was built up , symbolised by Pařížská street which opened a view of the Letná hill from the Old Town Square across the river Vltava. The spectacular boulevard engulfed the Wood Square outside the Altneuschul as well as picturesque old houses of the Moscheles and Wedeles families, the Three Wells Square and the Renaissance palace of Jacob Bassevi, Jewish butchers' shops with the Great Court Synagogue, New Synagogue and the ritual bath in Josefovská street, and Šmilesova and old Maiselova streets.

All that remained of the former Jewish Town were traces of the original thoroughfares in the groundplan of the network of streets, and some of the oldest monuments. What was left untouched was the centre of the ghetto with the Jewish Town Hall, the Altneuschul and the High Synagogue. The most authentic original setting was preserved in the Old Jewish Cemetery with the Klausen and Pinkas Synagogues at its end. The Maisel and Spanish Synagogues remained somewhat out of the way in the new housing project. While many of the ghetto's historical buildings were demolished, artistic monuments of its old synagogues were preserved in the Jewish Museum which was founded during the reconstruction in 1906 as one of the oldest Jewish museums in Central Europe.

Franz Kafka was born on July 3, 1883, in a house at the corner of Maiselova and Kaprova streets, almost exactly on the border of two quarters, which seemed to predestine the antagonism of his life and writings. He learned to know the ghetto in his childhood and experienced its demolition as well as the construction of the new quarter, which he recalls in his oft quoted recollection: "Living within us are still those dark corners, mysterious corridors, blind windows, dirty backyards, noisy pubs and closed inns. We walk down broad streets of the newly built town. But our steps and looks are uncertain. We still tremble within, like in the old lanes of poverty. Our hearts know nothing about the new sanitation. The unhealthy Jewish Town within us is much more real than the hygienic new town around." Franz Kafka's bust at the corner of his native house was made by sculptor Karel Hladík in 1967.

Ghetto in the 20th century

As a consequence of the Josephine educational reform and Germanising efforts of the Austrian government, most Czech Jews naturally adopted the German language from the late 18th century as a necessary prerequisite to their assimilation. Although in the 1840s some Jewish writers made attempts at a Czech-Jewish cultural and political rapprochement, their efforts went unappreciated on either side. Only in the 1870s, in connection with the growing immigration of Jews from the Bohemian countryside to Prague, an increasing number of Jewish associations and institutions came to exist with the aim of achieving also Czech-Jewish cultural assimilation. By the late 19th century the great majority of Prague Jews considered the Czech language their official tongue. Many of them took an increasingly significant part in supporting the Czech national movement in cultural as well as political terms.

Nevertheless, German still kept its privileged position as a common language of the multilingual Austrian monarchy in the field of culture and particularly in modern literature in the early 20th century. Prague German literature, whose authors were mainly Jewish, has gained world renown through the works by Franz Kafka, Franz

Werfel, Oscar Baum, Ludwig Winder and many others. Jewish writers and translators such as Arnošt Kraus, Otokar Fischer, Otto Pick, Rudolf Fuchs, Max Brod or Pavel Eisner played an important role as mediators between the two cultural spheres and their traditions.

In the Czechoslovak Republic which was declared on October 28, 1918, members of all the Jewish movements and organisations as well as representatives of modern culture supported the new state and created its new cultural orientation. The promising process aimed at a cultural transformation of Czech Jewry was cut prematurely and violently twenty years later by the Munich Accords of September 30, 1938, and the invasion of Nazi troops and declaration of the Protectorate of Bohemia and Moravia on March 15, 1939.

Immediately after the occupation, the Nazis banned the handling of Jewish property which could be taken over only by German custodians, becoming the Nazis' means of control over significant economic posts in the Protectorate. Jews were first excluded from legal and medical practices, from all spheres of public life and administration, and later from all the other professions, associations and organisations. Jewish children

17

were banned from attending all types of school. Jews were forbidden to move and travel, use the majority of public transport, go to restaurants, cafés and theatres, own and use phones and go out at night after eight. They had to surrender their radios, were forbidden to buy and read papers, and allowed to shop only in selected stores and at selected hours. They were not entitled to receive most of the food, fruit and tobacco rations. Their identity cards were marked with the letter "J" and from September 1941 they had to wear a yellow star with the inscription "Jude" on the left side of their chest.

This is when the new district lived through the old and ever-repeating tragic history of persecutions, pogroms and expulsion, which was even more horrifying because it happened in the mid-20th century and was greater than ever before. "During the last war, by a twist of fate, Prague Five became a ghetto again. The narrow crooked lanes were full of marked Jews again, and again the town was overcrowded. Again, the Jewish Town Hall, which had been standing as a mere monument for almost a hundred years, came to life. Again, the entire Jewish element was centralised forcefully, and again it was forbidden to reside anywhere but in Prague Five ... which resumed a ghetto character with all its respective attributes. Life was moved to the street again. The street could feel, hear and see and knew everything unfailingly. The terrible word 'transport' spread with unbelievable speed across each and every street, moving in each and every apartment and upsetting local inhabitants continuously from 1941 to 1945 ..." Hana Volavková wrote.

Deportations of Jews from Prague started as early as October 1941 with five transports of a thousand people each to the ghetto of Lodz. Only 260 persons survived to return after the war. By the spring of 1945, almost 45,500 citizens of Jewish origin were deported from Prague to Terezín and other concentration and extermination camps — 38,000 did not survive. Many others were arrested before deportation, committed suicide or died when attempting to escape or in resistance fights. Many of those who managed to leave the country in time perished while fighting Fascism on all fronts of World War II.

After World War Two, it was extremely difficult to restore the life of Prague's Jewish community that had been reduced to some 10 %. Many of the survivors who returned to Czechoslovakia travelled on to Western Europe, America or Israel to take part in building up a free Jewish state. After the Communist coup in 1948, the Jews were again barred from the political, economic and cultural life, and many of them jailed. A new hope of restoring the Jewish communal life emerged only with the revolution of November 1989. The almost deserted Jewish Town now begins to teem with numerous visitors, shops and cafés, becoming lively again.

This well-known statue of Rabbi Loew was made in 1910 by sculptor Ladislav Šaloun, who also designed John Huss' monument at the Old Town Square. The Old Town's new Town Hall was built at the time of reconstruction on the verge of the Old and Jewish Towns; this is why the artist chose the personality of Rabbi Loew as a symbol of Prague's ghetto for the Town Hall's facade. While making the statue, Šaloun was inspired by a legend of Rabbi Loew's death. Unable to approach the almost hundred-year-old scholar who was always absorbed in the study of Holy books, Death hid in a rose which was offered to the Rabbi by his unsuspecting granddaughter. The sculptor wrote about the statue: "Just as the beautiful child caused the death of Rabbi Loew with her sweet smelling flower, the new free time involuntarily crushed the old relics of the past by the spirit of its young life, thus ending the existence of Prague's ghetto."

19

At one time the Altneuschul dominated its surroundings by its height and size; today it is lost in the shadow of tenement houses in Pařížská street. According to legend, the synagogue was protected against fire in the ghetto by the wings of angels changed into doves. According to another folk tale, the remains of Golem, the artificial creature made of clay and brought to life by Rabbi Loew, are deposited in the synagogue.

THE ALTNEUSCHUL

The Altneuschul (Old New Synagogue) is now the oldest monument of Prague's ghetto. The origin of this house of worship is undoubtedly related to the foundation of the Old Town in the early 13th century, which called for an influx of new inhabitants as well as vivid building activities. It is probably at that time that the settlement in the area of Prague's ghetto experienced changes, too. In addition to the oldest housing quarters near the Altschul, the ghetto's inhabitants and new settlers concentrated in the vicinity of the Altneuschul which soon became the very centre of the Jewish Town. In 1254 Přemysl Ottokar II granted his privileges to the Jews of Bohemia, offering also to protect their houses, cemeteries and synagogues. To boot, the Prague Jewry obviously obtained permission to build a new synagogue, and to do so, to use the masons who were building the nearby monastery of St. Agnes.

Today the Altneuschul is a unique specimen of the mediaeval twin-nave type of synagogue. The oldest examples of this type were the Romanesque synagogue in Worms dating from the late 12th century (destroyed on November 9, 1938, and restored in 1960), and the early Gothic synagogue in Regensburg dating from the early 13th century (destroyed on February 21, 1519). The same is the disposition of the late Gothic synagogue in Kazimierz in Cracow from the early 15th century. The choice of the twin-nave type for mediaeval synagogues was not accidental. The same disposition was preferred, in mediaeval architecture, when building representative rooms for profane use, such as castle and town halls, refectories and capitular halls in monasteries, but also parlours in private houses, preserved in the Old Town of Prague from as early as the 12th century. It is also this twin-nave disposition which differentiated the synagogue from the contemporary ecclesiastical sacral buildings characterized by the central longitudinal orientation and an odd number of naves. At the same time, the twin-nave disposition better suited the arrangement of the interior where a platform with a pulpit (bimah, almemar) stood, and the hall-like space made it easier to arrange the pews along the peripheral walls. The disposition was probably originally influenced by ritual gatherings which had been organised in older times in dual-nave halls of private houses.

The interior of the Altneuschul is vaulted with six fields of five-ribbed vaulting supported by two hexagonal pillars. Bulky plastic ribs growing out of peripheral walls, and thick pillars form a tectonic framework of the building which is a great example of the constructional principles of Early Gothic architecture. The use of five-part vaulting made it possible to space more regularly narrow windows whose original number accorded with the symbolic number of the twelve tribes of Israel. The simple ribs are enlivened with relief decorations of vegetation motifs on brackets, capitals and vaulting joints. In this respect, the most advanced artistically is the decoration of the tympanum of the Holy Ark, featuring grapevine motifs, while the decoration of the tympanum of the entrance portal still suppresses the affinity with Nature on behalf of the symbolic stylization. The masonry decorations of ribs and the entrance portal also serve as the main means of dating the building, since no direct documents concerning its origin are available. Because of a close relation of this decoration to that of many early Gothic buildings in Bohemia (Prague's monastery of St.Agnes, monasteries in Zlatá Koruna and Vyšší Brod, Bezděz Castle and the parish church in Kolín), we may place the origin of the Altneuschul in the last quarter of the 13th century.

The middle part of the main room between the two pillars is occupied by a raised platform with a lectern for reading the Torah aloud, called bimah or almemar, which is separated from the surrounding space by a late-Gothic grillework with the motif of ogee arch. The protected area of the bimah is used only for the reading of the Torah and preaching; its traditional position in the middle of the room makes it possible for all the congregants to hear the text in the best possible way. The Altneuschul still uses the original arrangement of the seats around the bimah and along the walls of the main nave, as used to be the custom in other synagogues, too. The Holy Ark or aron ha-kodesh, where the Torah scrolls are kept, is situated in a niche in the centre of the eastern wall. The Ark consists of two Renaissance columns on volute brackets and a ledge dating from the 16th century. The decoration of the main room is complemented with numerous bronze chandeliers hanging down from suspended beams of the bimah grillework, as well as reflected sconces hung on the walls. Two early Baroque money-boxes placed in the southern vestibule used to keep Jewish taxes concentrated here from all over the kingdom.

The spiritual meaning of the Altneuschul's interior is manifested in the inscriptions and abbreviatures apparent on the walls, which are the only decoration of the room, e.g. in the vestibule we can read the quote of the last but one verse of Kohelet (12:13): "Fear God and keep his orders because this is all what man is"; the verse is what the visitor sees when both entering and leaving the synagogue. In the front part of the vaulting on the eastern wall of the main nave, the following quote in an abbreviated form can be read: "I always make God stand in front of my face" (Psalm 16:8) and the Talmudic saying of Rabbi Eliezer: "Know before whom you are standing . . ." reminding the congregants of constant presence of God and promoting concentration of mind at prayer. Other abbreviated quotes are inscribed on the opposite western wall, e.g. "Stand back from evil and do good" (Psalm 34:15).

The Altneuschul has always been much revered by Prague's ghetto inhabitants as well as foreign communities and is associated with a number of tales and legends. Among the historical events, the congregation especially remembers the victims of the Easter pogrom of 1389 when many ghetto dwellers were killed in this synagogue. An elegy (selicha) composed by Prague's rabbi-to-be and poet Avigdor Kara to commemorate the event whose eye-witness he was has been read every year on the Day of Atonement until today. As the Altneuschul has always been the Prague Jewry's main house of worship, its rabbis included the most outstanding personalities and preachers such as Eliezer Ashkenazi, Mordecai ben Abraham Jaffe, Judah Livah ben Bezalel and his foremost pupil Yom Tov Lipmann Heller renowned for his excellent commentary on the Mishnah. Later on, also Rabbi Ezechiel Landau, the last great authority of the traditional Rabbinical culture, was active there followed by Shelomo Judah Rapoport, outstanding representative of the Prague Haskalah movement.

Unlike the majority of the other synagogues in the Jewish Town, the Altneuschul has never become part of the surrounding housing scheme. It is probably due to its isolated position and solid construction that the synagogue avoided fires and other serious damage. An extensive reconstruction of this house of worship took place as late as 1883, according to the purist design by architect Joseph Mocker. A more thorough restoration was made in 1921—26 under the supervision of the State Office of Monuments Preservation; old plaster was renewed and the peripheral masonry examined. The last restoration so far took place in 1966—67.

The Altneuschul's original name was the New or Great Synagogue (Schul); the name Old New (Altneu in German) came into use only after other synagogues in the ghetto were erected in the late 16th century. Another explanation of its name is offered by one of the Jewish legends. The foundation stones for the construction of the Altneuschul are said to have been brought by angels from the destroyed Holy Temple in Jerusalem, "under the condition" (al-tenai in Hebrew) that they would be returned when the Temple is restored.

The Altneuschul is a simple rectangular building with a high saddle roof and late Gothic gables, and oriented in the usual eastern direction. The peripheral masonry is reinforced with low supporting pillars, opening with narrow pointed windows. The main building is on three sides surrounded by low annexes serving as a vestibule and a nave for women. The latter is connected with the synagogue's main room only with narrow slit openings in the wall to make it possible for the women to hear a service. The floor of the vestibule and main nave is somewhat lower than the level of the surrounding terrain, to accord with the tradition and to signify humility. (right)

The interior decoration of the Altneuschul is complemented with a high banner attached to the western pillar of the main nave. The privilege to carry the banner of their own as a symbol of independence was granted to the Jews of Prague by Charles IV in 1357. The banner was altered to its present form in 1716 under Charles VI on the occasion of celebrating the birth of his son, Archduke Leopold. The centre of the banner bears the Star of David containing a Jewish hat which was the sign of the Prague Jewry for centuries. (right)

The tympanum of the entrance portal leading to the synagogue's main nave is decorated with a relief of grapevine growing out of a stone with branches winding in a spiral, where numerical symbols are also applied. The wine shrub grows out of twelve roots, its branches carrying twelve grapes symbolising the twelve tribes of Biblical Israel. (left)

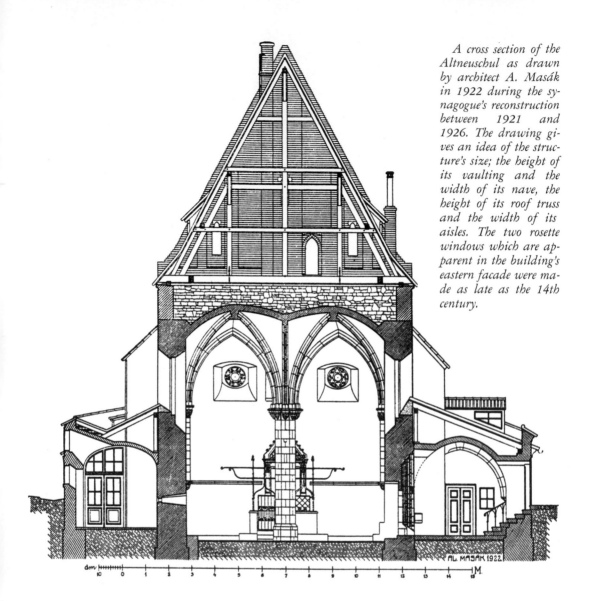

A cross section of the Altneuschul as drawn by architect A. Masák in 1922 during the synagogue's reconstruction between 1921 and 1926. The drawing gives an idea of the structure's size; the height of its vaulting and the width of its nave, the height of its roof truss and the width of its aisles. The two rosette windows which are apparent in the building's eastern facade were made as late as the 14th century.

The Torah scrolls are kept in a case called aron ha-kodesh in Hebrew (Holy Ark) which is situated beside the bimah, as the most important element of every synagogue's equipment. The ark is located in a niche in the eastern wall facing Jerusalem and is approached on a couple of steps lined with parapets on both sides. The door of the ark is covered with an embroidered curtain (parochet) and drapery (kaporet) above, both of which are decorated with traditional Jewish symbols such as the crown, a pair of lions or two columns and other motifs commemorating the Holy Temple of Jerusalem. In front of the Ark the eternal light (ner tamid) is hanging and a stone pulpit (amud) is situated on its right side; it is from here that the cantor conducts the service. The pulpit is also somewhat lower than the level of the adjacent floor in order to fulfil the words of Psalm No.130: "I call you from the depth, oh Lord." The shiviti tablet attached to the pulpit and bearing the introductory line of Psalm 16:8 ("I always make God stand in front of my face") helps the cantor concentrate his mind on prayers. (right)

The most outstanding Rabbi of Prague's Jewish community in the last century was Shalomo Judah Leib Rapoport (1790—1867) who belonged among the prominent personalities of the Jewish Enlightenment and was one of the founders of the New Age „Jewish studies" (Wissenschaft des Judentums). His main writings were a set of biographies of old Rabbinical authorities and an unfinished Talmudic encyclopaedia. Rapoport became Chief Rabbi of Prague in 1840 and shortly afterwards his portrait was painted by Prague's Antonín Machek, a well-known portrait artist of the Prague Enlightenment society.

THE SERVICE

The synagogal service consists of prayers, and of reading of Biblical text from the Torah and its explanation. The service is conducted by a cantor or hazzan who reads the prayers aloud. The daily prayers are divided into morning ones (shacharit), afternoon (minha) and evening ones (maariv). While praying in the morning, men wear white prayer shawls (tallit) with fringes reminding of God's commandments, and attach tefillin — leather cases containing Biblical injunctions on the forehead and the left arm. As for prayer books, Siddur is used for weekday prayers and Mahzor for individual festivals.

The Torah (Five Books of Moses) is the basis of Judaism as well as the main subject of synagogal liturgy. The service therefore culminates by reading the respective weekly portion of the Torah aloud but only provided that a minyan is present, i.e. if at least ten men of Jewish faith assemble. The Torah scroll is divided into 54 weekly portions which are read throughout the year to complete the entire cycle and start anew on the autumn festival of Simhat Torah. The respective weekly portion (sidrah) is read especially during Sabbath morning services,

a smaller part on festivals and during the morning service on Mondays and Thursdays.

During the service, the enfolded and adorned Torah scroll is taken out of the Holy Ark; then the Torah is carried around the bimah amidst the congregants who pay it hommage. Then it is taken to the bimah and put on the pulpit covered with an embroidered coverlet. There the Torah scroll is ceremonially undressed, and its silver adornments, mantle and binder removed. Usually, three men participate in reading the Torah, one of them pointing the text with a silver pointer, the second-usually the hazzan-reading aloud, and the third following and checking out the reading according to the printed text. On Saturdays, seven men are invited to read one after another, with an eighth reading a respective part of the Haftarah (Books of Prophets). When the reading of sidrah is over, the scroll is folded, firmly bound with the binder, dressed in the mantle and adorned with finials and a shield. Then the Torah is carried again by the worshippers around the bimah and deposited back in the aron ha-kodesh.

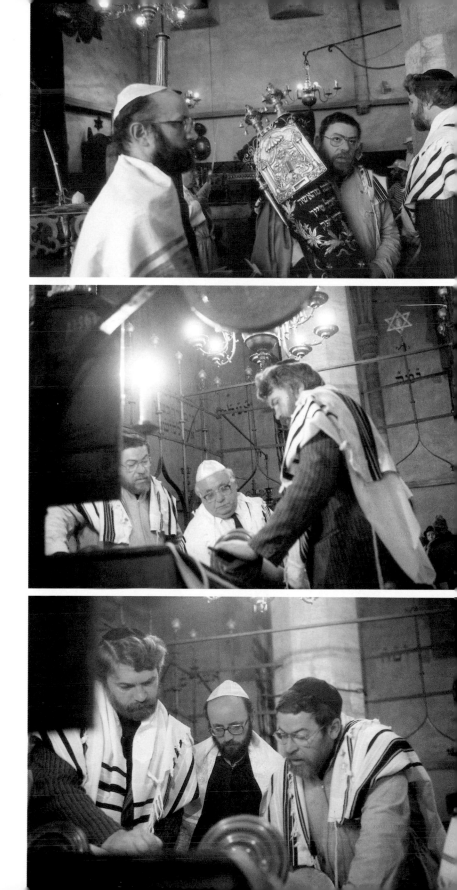

A picture from the early 20th century shows the interior of the Pinkas Shul after the reconstruction of 1862 when the floor of the main nave was considerably raised with made-up ground, a new ark replaced the old one, and benches in rows were added. A flag of the mystic and Kabbalist Shelomo Molcho was kept in the synagogue for centuries (it used to be hanging on the left of the aron ha-kodesh). Molcho's followers brought it to Prague after he was burnt at the stake in Mantua in 1532.

THE PINKAS SYNAGOGUE

The private prayer house of the Horowitz family was first mentioned in a document dating from 1492. It was then still a small structure at the edge of the Old Jewish Cemetery, forming a part of the tenement house called „At the Coats-of-Arms". In 1519 the ambitious Aharon Meshullam Horowitz inherited the house. It was he — according to the inscription on a tablet in the synagogue's anteroom — who had the present Pinkas Synagogue built in 1535 in place of the old prayer house. The name Pinkas Shul came into use in the late 16th century, most likely inspired by Aharon Meshullam's grandson Rabbi Pinkas Horowitz of Cracow.

The synagogue's high one-nave space is vaulted with the late-Gothic reticulated vaulting. The intersecting ribs cut the vaulting with contrasts of light, unifying and dynamising the space of the building. The thin peripheral masonry is reinforced with drawn-in buttresses among which five high stone windows are situated. As at the Altneuschul, the seats were originally arranged along the peripheral walls and turned to the platform from where the Torah was read in the centre of the room. The stylish character of the synagogue was enhanced by the rich stone-cut decoration on the aron ha-kodesh in the eastern wall, and on the bimah. The prevailing late-Gothic elements of the structure, however, are pervaded by a number of Renaissance motifs, the

most advanced of which is the decoration on the entry portal to the main nave, executed in unusually pure forms of the early Renaissance.

The deep level of the synagogue and insufficient inundation control in the area caused repeated flooding. After the floods of 1758 and 1771, the damaged aron ha-kodesh and bimah were restored in Baroque style. In 1838 the synagogue got a new tin case to keep the Torah scrolls, and in the 40s the old seats were replaced by new ones. After the flood of 1860, the floor in the main nave and anteroom was raised with made-up earth almost 1,5 metres high, the Baroque decoration of the aron ha-kodesh removed and the whole interior modernised.

The efforts to reconstruct the Pinkas Synagogue began as early as the 1920s when the first probes of the made-up earth were carried out and fragments of the original floor discovered. The principal reconstruction of the synagogue, however, was not done until the 1950s when the made-up ground was removed, original plaster uncovered and the ark, bimah and entrance portal restored. Between 1954 and 1959 the interior of the Pinkas Synagogue was turned into the memorial for the 77,297 Bohemian and Moravian victims of the Holocaust. The names arranged according to communities, and family names were inscribed on the walls of the main nave, balcony and anteroom. Implanted in their original milieus, the victims' names lost the anonymity of figures, reacquiring a human face. The combination of a historical building and the neighbourhood of the Old Jewish Cemetery put them together with generations of their ancestors.

Between 1607 and 1625 the synagogue was enlarged with an extended late-Renaissance additional building with a side nave for women, balcony and a spacious anteroom, all designed by the builder of the ghetto Tsoref Goldschmied de Herz. The facade of the new structure was articulated with a number of semicircular windows, as well as the main portal faced the inner yard which formed a sort of small Renaissance court until adjacent houses were demolished during the reconstruction of the ghetto.

Although the position of a synagogue in the vicinity of a cemetery is quite unusual, the Pinkas synagogue was built close to the Old Jewish Cemetery for lack of space in the ghetto. (above)

The one-nave space of the Pinkas Synagogue has a reticulated vaulting with high narrow ribs. The late-Gothic structure, however, is pervaded with a number of early-Renaissance elements, buttresses are decorated with fluting resembling Renaissance pilasters. The vaulting is ornamented with plastic Renaissance rosettes and a painted imitation of Renaissance stuccowork inspired by fashionable Italian models. (down)

The platform for reading of the Torah (bimah, almemar) is shifted somewhat toward the east due to the longitudinal layout of the building whose entrance is situated in its western part. The bimah was originally decorated with blind late-Gothic tracery with motifs of ogee arch. During the reconstruction in 1775 the stonecut decoration was removed and the bimah was covered with red marble stuccowork. To decorate the bimah, Joachim Popper donated a forged Roccoco grillework in 1793 which included a motif of the six-pointed star with a Jewish hat — an emblem of Prague's Jewish community.

The archaeological research of the Pinkas Synagogue in the 1970s discovered in the underground vaulted rooms with remnants of old wells and a ritual bath — mikveh — which made use of a permanent water supply in the neighbourhood. According to the preserved walls and ceramics, the ritual bath most likely dates from as early as the 15th century, belonging to the oldest documents of the Jewish settlement in the area.

A view of Rabínská street which was the main north-south thoroughfare of the ghetto. On the left side, one may see the corner of the Jewish Town Hall and the western facade of the Altneuschul. This is how the centre of Prague's ghetto with the original land coverage looked before the reconstruction. Photographed by Jindřich Eckert around 1900.

THE JEWISH TOWN HALL

No old information is available on the origin of the independent building of the Town Hall in Prague's ghetto. Nevertheless, since the earliest times Jewish communities in the diaspora enjoyed an autonomy through an elected council of elders, which decided all important matters of the community and represented the latter in relation to the ruler or the Town. An influential institution of the autonomy was the Rabbinical Court dealing with family law and litigation within the community.

The Jewish Town Hall was first mentioned as an independent building in documents dating from 1541. This building is believed to have been situated in the same place as the Town Hall of today, in the very centre of the Jewish Town. Its Renaissance reconstruction, however, could be carried out only after 1564 when more than twenty years of persecution of Prague Jewry under Ferdinand I were over. In 1567, his successor Maximilian II issued a decree promising that the Jews would not be expelled from Prague. In 1568 Mordecai Maisel (1528—1601) started to build the High Synagogue with which the Town Hall was closely tied. Thus the Town Hall was probably constructed either concurrently or a little later. Mordecai Maisel undoubtedly contributed financially to the construction of the new Town Hall, which was built by the Italian architect Pancratius Roder. Vaulted cellars and vaultings of the rooms situated in the northwestern corner of the building are remnants of the original Renaissance Town Hall. In this way the Jewish Town obtained a Town Hall of its own, in the second half of the 16th century, as a symbol of the newly strengthened independence and legal autonomy.

Despite the sufferings brought about by the Thirty Years War, Prague Jewry retained their privileges and around the mid-17th century, the Jewish community of Prague became one of the largest Jewish communities in Europe. In the last year of the Thirty Years War the Jews participated in the defence of the Old Town against the Swedish army which occupied Hradčany and the Lesser Town. As a reward for their brave assistance in fortifying the town and extinguishing fires, Prague's Jewish community was granted the right by Ferdinand II in 1648 to use a Swedish cap in the middle of the Star of David as its emblem. The Town Hall was burned down in the big fire on June 21, 1689, but was restored in the same year by the Baroque architect of Prague Paul Ignaz Bayer. During the expulsion by Maria Theresa in 1745—48, the Town Hall became delapidated and burned down once again in the fire of 1754. It is only in 1763—65 that it was rebuilt to its present form in the late Baroque style by Prague's designer Joseph Schlesinger. During the reconstruction, a memorial document was placed in the turret, recalling the loan of 200,000 guldens which helped restore the Jewish Town within eleven years. The Jewish Town Hall has retained its present form of a small late Baroque palace with a richly articulated facade, attic roof and dormer gables surmounted by a picturesque turret with a gallery and decorative Rococo railings.

As it has been for centuries, the Town Hall today is still the residence of Jewish autonomy — the Federation of Jewish Communities in the Czech Republic and the Jewish Community of Prague. Also the Rabbinate and a number of other religious, cultural and social institutions of the Jewish community reside here. A library is situated there as well as editorial offices of Jewish periodicals and a publishing house but one may also find lists of all Jewish citizens who were deported and perished during World War II, and the seat of the Terezín Initiative associating former prisoners of the Terezín ghetto.

The Rococo emblem situated over the side entrance to the Town Hall from Maiselova street bears the old sign of Prague's Jewish community, i.e. the Star of David (Magen David) with a pointed Jewish hat and the inscription 1765 — the year in which the reconstruction of the Town Hall was completed.

37

There was probably a tower clock on the Jewish Town Hall as early as in the second half of the 17th century. In its present form, the turret was built after the fire in 1754 and it was equipped with a new clock with Roman numerals and a bell. Another clock with Hebrew numerals whose hands revolve from right to left just like a Hebrew text is read, was at the same time placed on the gable of the front opposite the Altneuschul. By means of an ingenious gear, however, both clocks are operated by a single machine constructed in 1764 by Sebastian Laudensperger, Prague's royal court watchmaker. Especially thanks to poet Guillaume Apollinaire, the Jewish clock "going backwards" became an enigmatic symbol of the Prague ghetto in modern poetry. (right)

The Altneuschul and High Synagogue along with the Jewish Town Hall have been the innermost core of the Jewish Town for centuries. (left)

During the reconstruction of the Jewish Town in 1908—09, the Town Hall was enlarged on the right side of the main entrance in Maiselova street. In the ceremonial room on the ground floor, there is now the kosher restaurant; common gatherings of community members are organised and festivals celebrated here, too.

The meeting room on the second floor is used for sessions of various Jewish clubs and youth associations. This is where lectures are held, lessons in Hebrew language given and Hanukkah and Purim festivals traditionally celebrated. (above right)

A picture from the early 20th century shows the eastern part of the room after the High Synagogue's interior was adjusted in the second half of the 19th century.

THE HIGH SYNAGOGUE

The construction of the High Synagogue was completed by primate Mordecai Maisel (1528—1601) in 1568, as historian David Gans reported. The synagogue was originally accessible from a room on the first floor of the Jewish Town Hall, serving probably as a meeting place for the Jewish Council of Elders and the Rabbinical Court. The synagogue's name is most likely derived from its unusual location on the first floor, also suggesting its exclusive and non-public characters. The construction was carried out by a builder of Italian or South Tyrolian origin, Pancratius Roder, and local bricklayers under foreman Rada.

The synagogue's room with an almost square groundplan, which is illuminated through high windows on the facade, looks remarkably light. The way the walls are articulated in three parts by flat pilasters on the lower part of the room corresponds with lunettes on the vaulting as well as the position of windows in the northern and, originally also, eastern walls. The regular modulation of the walls enhances a good arrangement of the Renaissance room as well as its central disposition. The bimah with a pulpit for the reading of the Torah was originally also situated in the middle of the room while seats were placed along the walls. During the synagogue's reconstruction after the fire in 1689, the new Holy Ark was built in and, probably, a narrow structure added on the synagogue's southern side, which served as a balcony for women.

During the reconstruction in 1883 by architect J. M. Wertmüller, the entrance to the synagogue from the Town Hall was abolished, an inner staircase built and the main room fitted with new facilities. During the reconstruction of the Jewish Town, the High Synagogue was made part of the new housing scheme in 1907, its entrances on the eastern facade were abolished and the existing entrance opposite the Altneuschul was made. The restoration in 1961 discovered remnants of the original red polychromy on the vaulting and in 1982 the original appearance of the Holy Ark was first discovered under paintings made throughout centuries.

In 1982 a new exhibition of synagogal textiles was opened for public as the most precious part of the Jewish Museum's collections. It includes several thousand synagogal curtains, draperies and Torah mantles and binders which had been collected from all the pre-war Jewish communities in Bohemia and Moravia. Prague's collection is unique especially because it presents a continuous development of synagogal textiles from the 16th to 20th centuries, coming from a single territory. Their number and outstanding quality show that the Czech lands used to be among the most significant regions of the Jewish art of Jewish embroidery.

The almost central space is vaulted with a high Renaissance vaulting with corner lunettes and a rich stucco decoration imitating the Gothic shape of ribs which show the way of adjusting new Renaissance forms to the local Gothic tradition. Fields between the lunettes are ornamented with large stucco rosettes while an eight-pointed mirror whose frame is decorated with mother-of-pearl is situated in the vaulting's centre. A large carved and gold-plated chandelier became part of the room's decoration only in the last century.

It has been a custom in central and eastern European Ashkenazic communities to hang embroidered curtains (parochet) and draperies (kaporet) in front of the enclosed ark for the Torah scrolls, as the most important part of the synagogue's decoration. The oldest and most significant centre of production of synagogal textiles was Prague's embroidery workshop, whose development can be followed continuously since the late 16th century. (right)

The synagogue was partly damaged by fire in 1689. During repairs in 1691, it was fitted with a new early Baroque stone Ark with combined columns on the sides, a symbol of the Torah crown (keter Torah) and an inscription cartouche. During the restoration in 1982, the Ark's original colourful polychromy imitating red and brown marble was discovered. (left)

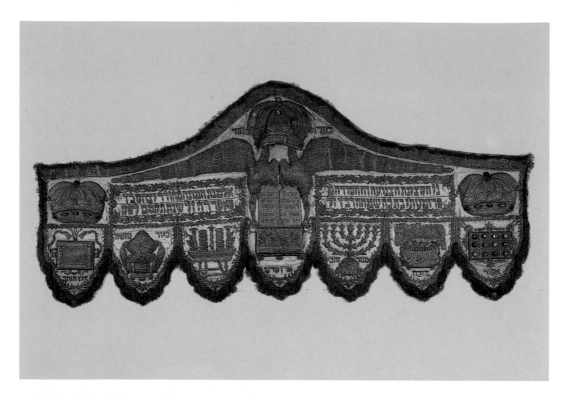

Prague's embroidered draperies (kaporet) from the high Baroque period are often decorated with symbols recalling the ceremonials of the Jerusalem Temple — the tablets with the Decalogue under the protection of cherubs, a seven-branched candelabrum, the High Priest's breast shield, an altar, incensory, wash-basin and a stand for sacrificial bread. (above)

The enfolded Torah scroll is tied with a binder (mappah) and dressed in an embroidered mantle (me'il) which enshrouds it, providing protection against damage while not in use. Mantles as well as curtains usually have in their upper part a Hebrew inscription with the name of donor and community, and the date of donation to the synagogue.

The most distinctive manifestation of the Jewish folk art are embroidered Torah binders (mappah). They were usually sewn at home on the occasion of birth of a son, and ornamented with a Hebrew inscription, stylised symbols of the Torah, wedding canopy (huppah) and flower and animal motifs.

A photograph from around 1905 offering a view of the western facade of the Maisel Synagogue after the neo-Gothic restoration, during which the entrance was shifted to Maiselova street and the synagogue made part of the housing scheme after the reconstruction.

THE MAISEL SYNAGOGUE

Towards the end of his life in 1590, primate Mordecai Maisel, who had so far been engaged in building public structures, bought a piece of land at the southern end of the ghetto to build a synagogue for his own use. In 1591 he obtained a special privilege from Emperor Rudolph II to do so, and a year later, on the festival Simhat Torah (Joy of the Torah), the synagogue was dedicated. It was built after a design by architect Judah Tsoref Goldschmied de Herz, the building works being conducted by Joseph Wahl.

Historian David Gans, Maisel's contemporary, says in his chronicle that the building was unusually impressive, and supported by twenty pillars. It was undoubtedly admired by contemporaries for the extent of its main nave. Maisel and his wife donated a rich treasure of synagogal textiles, mantles and curtains to the synagogue. It also served as a keeping place for a special banner which Maisel ordered made for himself on the basis of the privilege granted by Rudolph II in 1592, designed as a flag of Prague's Jewish community and kept at the Altneuschul. In the Renaissance period, the synagogue of Mordecai Maisel was the largest and most impressive house of worship in the Jewish Town.

The building was reportedly burnt down totally in the ghetto fire in 1689. It seems that the vaulting fell through and only the masonry of the pillars and peripheral walls were spared. By 1691, nothing but the eastern part of the structure was restored. Considering the original number of twenty pillars, out of which only fourteen have survived, to be part of the existing building, the synagogue must have been reduced approximately by one third of its original length. The original groundplan was surmounted by a new main nave and side naves for women with one-storey galleries.

The Maisel Synagogue was eventually restored in the last century, first in 1862—64 by architect J. M. Wertmüller, and again within the framework of the reconstruction of the Jewish Town in 1892—1905 in the neo-Gothic style as designed by architect Alfred Grott. When the network of streets was changed, the main entrance was moved to the western facade where a vestibule was built, designed by architect E. Králíček.

After the war, a depository of the Jewish Museum found its residence in the Maisel Synagogue. In 1963—64 plaster in the interior was restored, and in 1965, a permanent exhibition of synagogal silver from Bohemian and Moravian synagogues was opened there. Although the collection of synagogal silver is far from being as large as the textile collection, it is still one of the largest collection of silver artefacts in Czechoslovakia. The oldest silver objects date from the late 16th century but most of them only from the second half of the 18th and early 19th centuries. This is because the silver of old or damaged cult objects was often reused for new silverware.

Two tablets with the Decalogue in the gable usually denote synagogues. They symbolise the Torah (Five Books of Moses) which was given to Moses by God on Mount Sinai as a basis of Judaism.

On the occasion of the restoration being completed in 1905, a marble plaque with an inscription commemorating Mordecai Maisel, founder of the synagogue, was installed. Another plaque bearing a similar inscription in Czech was built in the synagogue's vestibule.

During the neo-Gothic restoration of the synagogue in the late 19th century, the vaulting was fitted with false ribs, new windows with coloured glass set in and accessories including the aron ha-kodesh were executed in the stylised Gothic style.

This unusual view of the Maisel Synagogue from the eastern side gives the best idea of what the building and its position in the ghetto's housing scheme looked like. At a time the eastern facade contained the main entrance of the synagogue from old Maiselova street. This part of the building is now lost amid a large block of tenement houses.

From the artistic point of view, Baroque, Rococo and Empire Torah shields are particularly interesting, including pairs of silver finials made by goldsmiths from Prague, Brno and Vienna.

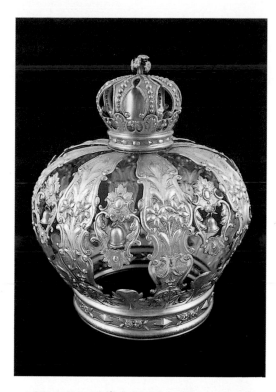

The largest part of the collection consists of silver Torah ornaments. The wooden rollers on the enfolded and dressed Torah scroll are adorned with a pair of silver finials (rimmonim) or a crown (keter) which is a symbol of the royal majesty of the Torah. A silver shield (tas) is hung on the front side of the scroll to mark the place where the scroll is opened. Silver pointers (yad), much varied in form, are used to point the text of the Torah, which a reader is forbidden to touch by hand.

The objects which are part of the Jewish Museum's collections, relating to the observance of the Sabbath include hanging Sabbath lamps, pairs of silver candle holders and silver kiddush cups for benediction over wine. Most interesting, however, are silver spice containers (besamim) of various forms, used for the Havdalah ceremony to conclude the Sabbath.

A photograph from the early 20th century recorded the eastern part of the interior of the Klausen Synagogue after adjustments made in the 1880s.

THE KLAUSEN SYNAGOGUE

The origin of the Klausen Synagogue also goes back to the Renaissance period of the ghetto. The term "Klausen" was originally used for three small buildings constructed by Mordecai Maisel at the border of the Old Jewish Cemetery to commemorate Emperor Maximilian II's visit to the Prague ghetto in 1571. One of them housed a synagogue, another a ritual bath (mikveh) and the third a renowned Talmudic school of higher learning (yeshiva) of Rabbi Loew. Like other monuments of the ghetto, these three buildings were destroyed by a great fire on June 21, 1689, which ravaged all of the 316 houses of the ghetto, most synagogues and public buildings. The fire triggered an effort by the authorities to reduce the size of the Jewish Town and this is why all the buildings had to be restored as soon as possible in order to prevent their demolition. The Klausen Synagogue, completed in 1694, was built thanks to Shelomo Chalish Kohen, superior of the preceding house of worship, in the same place where the destroyed "klausen" were situated.

The basic disposition of the Klausen Synagogue consists of a lengthwise hall covered with vaulting broken by four pairs of lunettes. These correspond with two rows of semi-circular vaulted windows placed on the southern side of the building facing the Old Cemetery. The walls are divided by pilasters carrying curved entablature surmounted by a strongly protruding cornice. The vast room of the ghetto's once largest synagogue is complemented with an original three-tiered Holy Ark built at the expense of Samuel Oppenheim in 1696. A picture dating from the middle of the last century shows that here as well a large oblong bimah was standing in the centre of the room, the pews being placed on the periphery of the main nave. The synagogue became the second main house of worship for Prague Jewry, also serving as a synagogue of Prague's Burial Society. Its Rabbis included outstanding representatives of the Jewish congregation, such as Eliezer Fleckeles, Samuel Kauder, Efraim Teweles, Baruch Jeiteles etc.

During the restoration of the synagogue by designer B. Münzberger in 1883—84, the western part of the building was extended and another broad part added. The vaulting was unified with renewed plaster decorations and the windows glazed with coloured panes. The exterior facades of the building were fashioned at that time, too. The interior was restored in 1960 and again in 1979—81, the restoration of the Baroque ark being made in 1983. One year later, a permanent exhibition of Hebrew manuscripts and prints was opened at the Klausen Synagogue.

For want of space, the Klausen Synagogue is also situated at the border of the Old Jewish cemetery. The building is marked by two tablets with the Decalogue atop the eastern gable; under the circular window situated in the centre of the facade, a tablet is set bearing a Hebrew inscription related to the reconstruction of the synagogue in 1694.

A money-box made of Slivenec marble in the form of a Baroque aspersorium and placed in the vestibule of the Klausen Synagogue is one of the few parts of the original equipment of the building. This is a reminder of the fact that the same bricklayers built synagogues as well as Baroque churches of Prague.

The Klausen Synagogue is now the only building giving an idea of what the other early Baroque buildings in the ghetto looked like, such as the Zigeuner, Great Court or New Synagogues. All of them were also built shortly after the fire in 1689 to replace older structures destroyed by the fire. (left)

ספר
צרי היגון

כושל יקימון שלין · ונרכים בושלות יאמץ
סגולת ספר צרי היגון · להשקים הנפש מדאבון
בסוב חמשת שיני רנן · להשביע רגוף מרעבון

נדפס ראשנ ק קריסונה · זה יותר מחמשי שנה · ולא נמצא
...תחלת הספר · הנותן אמרי
...אמרתי להדפיסו עוד
...ולתפארת

נדפס שנית בפה הזק פראג

ע"י האחוק"ק כה"רר יעקב בר גרשון ב"ק ז"ל

In the early 16th century, the ghetto's oldest printing house of Gershom Kohen started work which continued for almost three centuries. Its prints are characterised by the high typographic and artistical levels, which are especially apparent in the decoration of full-page title pages. One of its original products, the book of benedictions entitled *Seder zemirot u-birkat ha-mazon* from 1514, has probably been preserved in a single copy. Well-known is the Prague editions of the Pentateuch from 1518 and 1530 and especially the so-called Prague Haggadah dating from 1526, with numerous woodcut illustrations. *(right)*

Gershom Kohen's printing house in Prague printed some of the numerous writings of Judah ben Bezalel alias Rabbi Loew (1512—1609), the leading scholar of the Renaissance ghetto. *(left)*

The last period of the development of Hebrew manuscript art is represented in Czechoslovakia by small but often richly decorated illuminated manuscripts of the Moravian school from the 18th and early 19th centuries. *(right)*

The Old Jewish Cemetery's romantic appearance has attracted visitors of Prague since the late 18th century. It later became a subject of many works by landscape painters of the Mánes and Haushofer schools. The photograph from about 1900 shows the way the cemetery looked with its lilac shrubs.

THE OLD JEWISH CEMETERY

Apart from the Altneuschul, the Old Jewish Cemetery is the most significant monument of Prague's ghetto and today probably the oldest and historically most important Jewish cemetery in Central Europe.

The Old Jewish Cemetery, however, was not the oldest burial ground of Prague Jewry. The oldest Jewish cemetery in Prague was situated in the Lesser Town in the vicinity of the castle, most likely somewhere near Újezd street. Prague's second Jewish cemetery was founded in the 13th century on the territory of what was to become the New Town, in the area between today's Spálená and Jungmannova streets. The cemetery which was also called "the Jewish Garden" served as a burial ground for not only Prague's Jewish dead but also Jewish communities in the country. It was abolished with advancing housing projects in the New Town in 1478.

Today's Old Jewish Cemetery was founded in the early 15th century, this time nearly in the centre of the ghetto. Despite the expansion and combination of individual areas, the cemetery's limited territory soon became insufficient for new burials. Since a religious custom forbids the destruction of old graves, new layers of earth were piled on top of one another for the dead to be buried. In some places there were finally as many as ten burial layers. The old tombstones were always raised on the surface which is how the typical dense cluster of stone stelae dating from different centuries came into existence.

The cemetery now holds almost 12,000 tombstones dated from 1439 to 1787 when a decree issued by Joseph II prohibited the further use of burial grounds in populated areas. Actually there were many more burials because plenty of small gravestones had sunk into the ground while others, particularly those made of wood, were destroyed in the course of time. The historical significance of the cemetery consists in inscriptions on tombstones that provide an important source of the history of Prague Jewry, as well as in the cultural and historical values of some prominent figures who are buried at the cemetery. It is also a unique monument of artistical and historical characters, and a valuable witness to the long-time development of Jewish sepulchral arts.

Prague's oldest Jewish tombstones dating from the 14th century were moved to the Old Jewish Cemetery from the excavation site at the abolished Jewish cemetery in Vladislavova street in 1866. Their fragments are built in a monument next to the eastern face of the Klausen Synagogue. In the early 15th century an oblong or square type of tombstone made of sandstone came into use, with inscriptions carved in high relief. Such headstones include the stela on the grave of Prague's Rabbi and poet Avigdor Kara (died on April 25, 1439) or the tombstone of Aharon Meshullam Horowitz (around 1470—1545), founder of the Pinkas Synagogue, or that of the proprietor of the first Hebrew press Mordecai Zemach (d. 1592), son of Gershom Ha-Cohen, who is buried at the cemetery together with his son Bezalel (d. 1589). Such gravestones were used at the Old Cemetery in minor variations until the early 17th century.

From the late 16th century, the production of tombstones began to make use of white and red marble and plaster relief lettering as well as various decorative elements. In that time, a whole system of tombstone design classification developed and functioned in various forms for full two centuries. Since around 1600 a new form of gravestone was in use, namely a large four-wall tomb which was usually built only above the grave of the most prominent figure of the community. A large surface of the face and side stones made it possible to render a longer text depicting the deceased person's significant deeds and charitable acts. The oldest tombs at the cemetery can be found on the grave of Mordecai Maisel (1528—1601), the Jewish Town's leading personality and principal investor of buildings in the Jewish Town during the Renaissance, and that of his contemporary, philosopher and thinker Judah ben Bezalel called Rabbi Loew (1512—1609). Other tombs mark the graves of Joseph Delmedigo of Candia (1591—1655), of Prague's Chief Rabbi Aharon Shimeon Spira (1600—1679), or that of Rabbi David Oppenheim (1664—1736) who concentrated the greatest collection of old Hebrew ma-

nuscripts and prints, while living in Prague.

Inscriptions on tombstones are written in square Hebrew lettering. The headline usually gives the name of the deceased as well as the name of his father while women's names also include the name of their husband; the date of death, sometimes even that of the burial. Inscriptions on mediaeval stones are usually very simple, in the 15th and 16th centuries also including information on the profession of the deceased, praising his outstanding abilities and moral qualities, especially his education and scholarship, mentioning also his position in the community and his charitable acts, and sometimes expressing the sorrow of survivors and their wishes for him to be rewarded in the after-world. Originally brief texts grew on Baroque tombstones into extended poetic compositions rich in metaphors and quotations from the Bible.

The last tombstone at the Old Jewish Cemetery is that of Moses, son of Lipman Beck, who died on May 17, 1787. During the sanitation reconstruction of the quarter of Josefov, the north-western section of the cemetery was demolished and in 1903, the tombstones from this area were built in the wall surrounding the "Nefeleh" mound outside the eastern facade of the Klausen Synagogue. The cemetery lot was encircled with a new wall designed by architect Bohumil Hübschmann in 1911.

The picture is part of the cycle of Burial Society Paintings dated from about 1780, showing the Society's activities and funeral rituals in 15 paintings. The paintings were originally supposed to decorate the Burial Society's gathering hall.

A view of the central part of the Old Jewish cemetery with a tomb of the Jewish Town's leading figure Mordecai Maisel (1528—1601) in the middle among rows of simple gravestones dating from the 16th to 18th centuries. An extended epitaph covers the tomb's front and rear tablets while the side ones hold inscriptions of a later date, recalling the tomb's reconstruction in 1725, after the return from exile in 1759, and in the mid-19th century.

The new ceremonial building of the burial society which is situated near the entrance to the Old Jewish Cemetery was built by architect J. Gerstl in place of an old mortuary between 1906 and 1908. The elaborate and articulate structure with a turret and covered entry staircase was built in pure neo-Romanesqe style out of argillite, the usual stone used for Prague's mediaeval structures. All the details of the building are marked by perfect craftsmanship — column footings and heads, as well as a balcony from which eulogies over the coffin used to be made; and a heavy oak door and forged grille. The main room in the first floor is fitted with a mosaic floor and marble wall lining. It was originally also decorated with wall paintings.

But the new ritual hall which is connected with the mortuary and a room for ritual cleaning of the dead did not serve its original purpose for too long. Funeral processions were dispatched from Josefov to the New Jewish Cemetery only until the early '20s. In 1926 the ritual building was rented by Prague's Jewish museum which used it for the third exhibition of its collections. After the war, a permanent exhibition of the Museum of Prague's Ghetto was opened there to expose monuments and the history of Prague's ghetto. Children's drawings from the Terezín concentration camp have been shown there since 1978. (left)

The gravestone of Hendel (d. 1628), daughter of Eberle Geronim and wife of Jacob Bassevi, is the only tomb at the Old Jewish Cemetery above a woman's grave. With its spectacular late-Renaissance decoration and huge size, however, it surpasses most tombstones of significant scholars and rabbis buried at the cemetery. Hendel Bassevi was noted for her charity and the support she provided to the poor in the ghetto. Her good qualities and noble acts are depicted in the extended inscription on the tomb's face and side tablets. The sculptures of sitting lions with a coat-of-arms at the head of the tombstone are a symbol of nobility. The proper coat-of-arms with an oblique stripe and three silver stars can be found in the emblem's centre in the middle of the tomb's side tablets.

The late-Renaissance tomb atop the grave of Judah ben Bezalel called Rabbi Loew (1512—1609) and his wife Pearl (d. 1609), daughter of Rabbi Shmuel, is the most sought-after gravestone at the Old Jewish Cemetery. The tombstone is divided in two parts with inscriptional cartouches, and decorated with reliefs of grapes and a split shield with a central superstructure with the relief of a two-tail lion, Rabbi Loew's emblem, with a pine cone at the end. Inscriptions continue on the tomb's rear wall and then on the side tablets. The top tablets hold inscriptions of a later date reminding of the reconstructions of the tomb in 1752 and 1815.

Rabbi Loew, Prague's MAHARAL, was born in 1512 in Posen in Poland. When he was young he studied in Prague under Rabbi Jacob Polak (1460—1541). It is there that he met Pearl. From 1553 he held the office of Moravian Chief Rabbi in Mikulov for twenty years but he gave up the prominent post in 1573 and moved to Prague where he became rector of the Talmudic school of higher learning which gained a considerable reputation under his leadership. In 1592 he was called to Posen to act as Chief Rabbi there. After five years, however, he returned to Prague in 1597 and finally obtained the office of Prague's Chief Rabbi which he held until his death. (left)

The central part of the cemetery holds three tombs on the graves of members of the Spira family of Rabbis. The oldest tomb, a huge Baroque one, marks the grave of Prague's Chief Rabbi Aharon Shimeon Spira (1599—1679) called also "Shimeon the Pious" or "Shimeon the Righteous" who held the office of Prague's Chief Rabbi for forty years and was regarded as a great expert in Mishnah and religious juridical literature. His learning and piety as well as the hardship he went through are described in an extended inscription on the tomb's faces and side walls which also hold carved allegorical depictions of his foes and a rare portrait of the Rabbi himself. (right)

At the entrance of the cemetery there are two gravestones dating from the late 17th century, which mark the graves of Prague's Jewish physicians of the Teller family. The marble tombstone in the front was erected atop the grave of Judah Loew Teller who died in 1697. (left)

From the late 16th century, tombstones were more often decorated with relief symbols and signs. Those are particularly general symbols inspired by Biblical and other traditional Jewish literature, such as the crown — a symbol of wisdom and learning, or the grape — a symbol of fertility and life. Other symbols relate to the origin, name or profession of the deceased. The symbol of blessing hands or a laver thus tells that the deceased person belonged to the Biblical priestly tribe Kohanim or their assistants Levites.

The deceased person's profession is most often symbolised by the sign of a tool typical for a certain trade or activities; scissors are most frequently depicted on the graves of tailors, doctors' graves are denoted with a medical lancet, a pharmaceutical mortar decorates apothecaries' graves while a book is a symbol used for the grave of a prayer reader or scholar. A peculiarity of the Old Jewish Cemetery, however, is the figure motif, most often a woman's figure depicted on the tombstones of young unmarried girls, whose meaning has not been fully explained so far.

Reliefs of animals mostly serve as symbols of the deceased person's name. The most frequent ones to be found at the cemetery are the lion which is a symbol of the name Judah or Arye, the deer depicts the name Zevi or Hirsch, wolf symbolises the name Zeev or Wolf, bear stands for Dov or Bär, fish can mean the surname Karpeles or Fischel. We can often find depictions of various birds symbolising e.g. the name Jonah (dove), Hahn (cock), Gans (goose), or the frequent woman's name Feigle (bird). Rarely found at the cemetery are reliefs of fox (denoting the surname Fuchs), pole-cat (Iltis) or mouse (Maisel). Depictions of mythical animals such as the lion with wings, Pegasus or griffin only have protective and decorative meanings.

An unusual view of the north-eastern corner of the cemetery where the original entrance gate used to be. This part of the cemetery holds mainly tombstones dating from the 18th century. On the left side of the alley we can find the small gravestone of Moses Lipman Beck who was buried on May 17, 1787, which was the last burial at the cemetery.

An alley leading up to the right goes to a small mound outside the eastern facade of the Klausen Synagogue. It was formed in place of the former Jewish hospital which had been founded by Mordecai Maisel in the late 16th century but burnt down in 1689. The mound is called "Nefeleh" ("miscarriage" in Hebrew) because from the early 18th century it was used as a burial ground for still-born babies or those who died within one month after their birth, for burial rules applying to them are different from those applying to the adult dead.

During the reconstruction of Prague's ghetto, the remains from graves situated in the abolished north-western part of the cemetery were moved to the mound, as well as some of the tombstones. A history of expropriation of the cemetery's marginal parts during the sanitation reconstruction of the ghetto is depicted in a memorial inscription on a modern tomb dating from 1903 which stands at the edge of the mound.

A photograph dating from about 1890 shows the newly built Spanish Synagogue among the houses adjacent to the Altschul at the corner of Vězeňská and Dušní streets.

THE SPANISH SYNAGOGUE

It is something of a paradox that the last large synagogal structure on the territory of the Jewish Town was built to replace its oldest synagogue. That was always considered to be the Old Synagogue (Altschul) which served as a house of worship for a small district separated from the ghetto throughout its existence. After the Easter pogrom of 1389 the Altschul was burnt down and demolished. It is reported that from the late 15th century it was used by Jewish exiles driven from Spain and Portugal. That is also testified to by special ancient prayers in use at the Altschul.

In 1837 reformed service was first introduced at the Old Synagogue and it was also here that synagogal music was played. Significant representatives of the rising Jewish studies were summoned here as preachers of the Association of Reformed Service, such as the well-known orientalist and specialist in Hebrew studies Leopold Zunz, preacher Michael Sachs and between 1846 and 1868 Professor Saul Isaac Kaemf. To assist in developing synagogal music, František Škroup, who composed the Czech national anthem and the first Czech opera was asked to work here between 1836 and 1845. In the '40s, the interior of the Altschul was modernised in neo-Gothic style.

Since the Old Synagogue, however, did not meet the needs of the growing Association of Reformed

Service, it was soon decided to erect a new building. The Altschul was torn down in 1867 and a new synagogue built in its place. It came into use in May 1868. The project was made by Prague's architect Vojtěch Ignác Ullmann, and the interior designed by architect Josef Niklas. The synagogue has a square central groundplan and a large dome above the middle part. On three sides, there are balconies on metal constructions, open into the main room. The interior was decorated between 1882 and 1893 according to a design by A.Baum and B. Münzberger. It includes a low stucco arabesque of stylised Islamic motifs which is richly gilded and polychromed in green, blue and red. The same decorative elements are used in the carved decoration of the door, organ, balcony railing and wall lining on the groundfloor. The windows, too, were filled with painted glass in 1882—1883. The perfectly finished ornamental decoration makes the whole space look uniform in style. Owing to the rich decoration in the Moorish style, the synagogue was called the Spanish.

Only in the late 1950s the Spanish Synagogue which was used as a warehouse during World War Two, was handed over to the Jewish Museum and at least partly restored in 1958—59. In 1960 the first permanent exhibition of synagogal textiles opened, remaining there until 1982.

The Spanish Synagogue's western facade is ascribed to architect V. I. Ullmann, designer of numerous neo-Renaissance buildings in Prague. The facade's centre holds two tablets with the Decalogue, a traditional designation of a synagogue.

A view of the eastern part of the Spanish Synagogue's main room shows the unusual design of the Holy Ark shaped as a high tabernacle inspired by Moorish architecture. (right)

The non-traditional Holy Ark with two bronze lions holding tablets with the Decalogue is part of the winter house of worship attached to the Spanish Synagogue in 1935 according to the design by architect Karel Pecánek, as the last synagogal structure built in Prague before World War Two. (left)

74

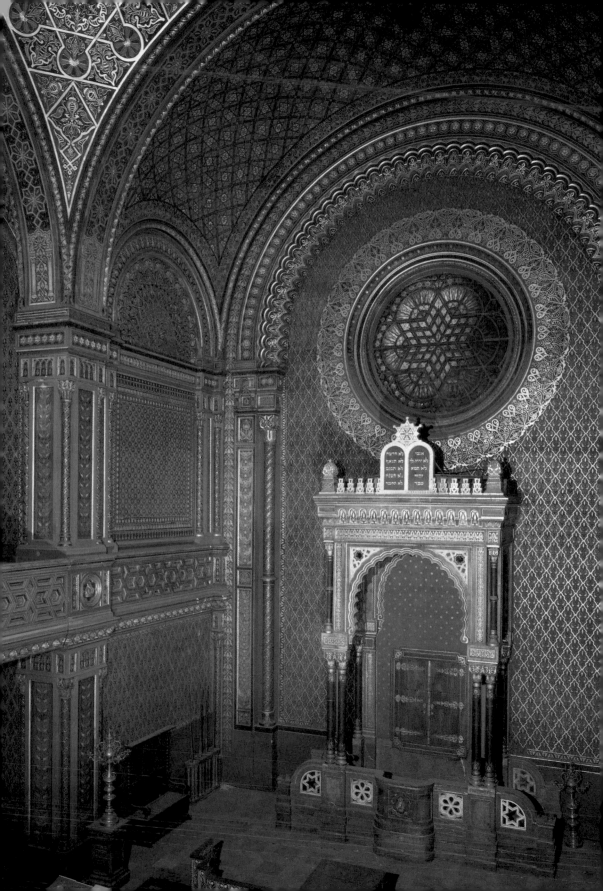

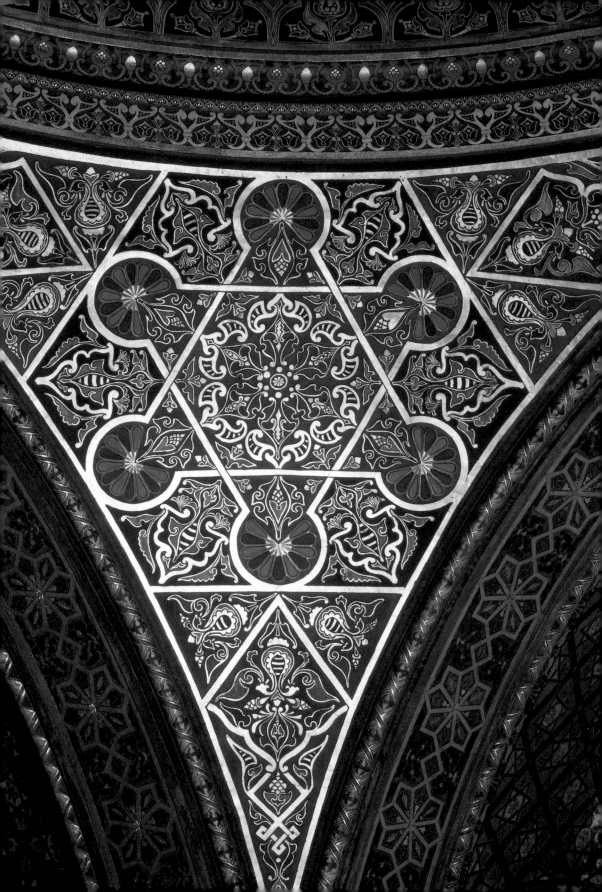

Large rosette windows in the synagogue's side walls were added in 1882-83. They are painted in yellow colour which makes the sun rays shining in look golden.

From the 1860s, the so-called Moorish lounge came into use in building new synagogues. It was inspired by mediaeval Islamic monuments on the territory of the Iberian peninsula, and commemorates the Golden Age of Jewish history in Moslem Spain. (left)

THE JUBILEE SYNAGOGUE

After a decision was taken that the Jewish Town was to be redeveloped by way of sanitary reconstruction, a society was established in 1898 to build a new synagogue that was supposed to replace the Zigeuner, Great Court and New Synagogues doomed for demolition. The society then financed the construction of a new synagogue built in Jeruzalémská street in the borough of the New Town in 1905—06 designed by Wilhelm Stiassny, the well-known Austrian architect. Building works were conducted by Alois Richter of Prague. In terms of architecture, the synagogue is an interesting specimen of a free Art Nouveau stylisation with ornamental features in the Moorish style. The facade was designed as a stately portico and the interior is given rhythm by two rows of arcade galleries placed over one another. The synagogue is still in use for religious services by Prague's Jewish community.

The decision to build the synagogue was taken at the time of the Silver Jubilee of Franz Joseph I's ascension to the Austrian throne, which is why it was called the Jubilee Synagogue in his honour.

The galleries are placed on depressed Islamic arches. The conspicuously lengthwise disposition of the synagogue is given rhythm by long rows of arcades placed over one another. *(right)*

The remarkable painted decoration of the synagogue, marked by Art Nouveau orientalism, was designed and made by painter František Fröhlich. The decoration of the interior is complemented by numerous chandeliers and wall lights inspired by the Islamic art of metal chiselling. *(left)*

THE OLD OLŠANY CEMETERY

When interment at the Old Jewish Cemetery in overcrowded Josefov was prohibited in 1787 for sanitary reasons, Prague's Jewish community began to use the former plague cemetery at Olšany as its main burial ground. The cemetery was established during the devastating plague epidemic in 1680 when some 3,000 dead from Prague's ghetto were buried there. The cemetery was re-used temporarily during the plague in 1713 and during the expulsion of the Jews from Prague in 1745—48. The cemetery was enlarged several times during the last century. It was soon approached by new tenement houses of the suburban quarter of Žižkov and, consequently, interment was prohibited there in 1890.

In over a hundred years, some 37,800 dead were buried at the Old Olšany Cemetery in Žižkov, including a number of significant representatives of Prague's Jewish community such as primate Israel Frankl Spira (1712—1791), head of Prague's Talmudic school Eleazar Fleckeles (1754—1826), the Moravian Landesrabbiner Nehemias Trebitsch (1799—1842) and Prague's Chief Rabbi Shalomo Judah Rapoport (1790—1867). A number of important scientific, cultural, social and economic personalities of Prague's Jewish community from the period of Enlightenment and emancipation included teacher Peter Beer (1755—1838), publisher Israel Moses Landau (1758—1829) and mathematician Jacob Koref (1790—1852). Founders of Prague's first industrial factories are also buried at the cemetery, such as Leopold Jerusalem (1789—1842), Aharon Beer Príbram (1781—1852) and Salomon Príbram (1808—1865), Leopold Lämmel (1790—1867) and Leopold Porges of Portheim (1781—1870).

The surrounding cemetery wall was torn down in 1958—60, tombstones were covered with earth and the majority of the cemetery's territory was changed into a park. Only the northern-most — the oldest — part of the cemetery with the most valuable tombstones in terms of history and design from the periods of classicism and Empire, and with the adjacent building of the former plague hospital was left untouched, to be surrounded by a new wall and restored in 1986—87. Between 1986 and 1989 a new television transmitter was erected on the site and the majority of the old cemetery's tombstones were dumped during excavations.

אל ויֹשים העין
לאמר הֹפה קֹבֹר

A view of the oldest part of the Old Olšany Cemetery where a lot of leading personalities of Prague's ghetto from the late 18th and early 19th centuries are buried. Two high tombstones on the right of the picture belong to nobleman Joachim Popper (d. 1795), a successful entrepreneur and philanthropist, and his wife.

The large neo-Renaissance ritual hall was built between 1891 and 1893 according to the design by architect B.Münzberger. In the 1920s, the eastern part of the cemetery was enlarged and in 1933 an urn grove with a functionalist ritual hall designed by Leopold Ehrmann was also established there.

THE NEW OLŠANY CEMETERY

The lot for a new Jewish cemetery in Nad vodovodem street was acquired by Prague's burial society in 1888. In the two years that followed, a cemetery wall and a house for a nightwatchman were built, and in July 1890 the first dead were buried there. In the fifty years between 1890 and 1940 almost 15,000 corpses were interred at the cemetery, including many significant personalities of economic life, science and culture.

Prominent figures of Prague's Jewish community buried there include Rabbis Saul Isaac Kaemf (1813—1892), Nathan Grün (1840—1913), Filip Bondy (1830—1907), Chief Rabbis dr.Nathan Ehrenfeld (1843—1912) and dr.Gustav Sicher (1880—1960), heads of Prague's Jewish community JUDr.August Stein (1854—1937) and dr.Ludvík Singer (1876—1931), and the founder of Prague's Jewish Museum dr.Salomon Hugo Lieben (1880—1967). Members of the families of entrepreneurs Petschek and Waldes are buried at the cemetery as well as the leading promoter of the Czech-Jewish movement Bohumil Bondy (1832—1907) and the well-known patron of Czech artists of the National Theatre generation, Alexander Brandeis (1848—1901).

Between 1890 and 1939 a lot of artistically valuable tombstones were erected at the cemetery. Many of them were designed by prominent architects Jan Kotěra (the tombs of the Elbogen family dating from 1901, Robitschl from 1902, the Perutz family from 1902 and 1904), Antonín Balšánek (the tomb of the Weltsch family dating from 1900), J. Fanta (the tomb of the Bondy family from 1907) and L. Ehrmann (the gravestone of L. Singer from 1931); as well as by well-known sculptors Jan Štursa (Max Horb 1907), Čeněk Vosmík and Emanuel Kodet. In this respect, too, the New Jewish Cemetery is a remarkable cultural monument documenting the development of funeral architecture and sculpture from historicising styles of the late 19th century, through the variety of artistic forms of the Art Nouveau, to the neo-classicism and functionalism of the 1920s and 1930s. *(above right)*

Significant personalities of modern art and literature buried at the cemetery include writers Franz Kafka (1883—1924), Josef Bor (1906—1979) and Ota Pavel (1930—1973), poets Hugo Salus (1866—1929), František Gottlieb (1903—1979) and Jiří Orten (1919—1941) at the urn grove, and painters Max Horb (1882—1907) and Jiří Kars (1880—1945).

A Glossary of Hebrew and Foreign Terms

Aggadah — literature dedicated to ethical-religious questions which are explained by means of narratives, parables and proverbs.

Almemar — Arabic term for a platform with a pulpit for the reading of the Torah, see Bimah.

Amud — pulpit for the hazzan, located on the right of the holy ark.

Aron ha-kodesh — holy ark at the eastern wall of the synagogue, serves for keeping the Torah scrolls.

Ashkenazic — mediaeval Hebrew term for "German"; conventional term used to designate the Jews originating from western and eastern Europe.

Bar mitzvah — son of divine commandment in Aramaic; a ritual of usherance of a boy of 13 into the congregation.

Bessamim — "spices"; decorative boxes where spices for the Havdalah ritual are kept.

Bimah — Greek term for an elevated rostrum with a pulpit for the reading of the Torah. It is situated in the synagogue's central or eastern part.

Ghetto — originally an Italian designation of an enclosed Jewish settlement separated from the other parts of town.

Golem — "imperfect, shapeless", artificial being according to legend, the most famous Golem was created and made alive by Rabbi Loew in Prague in the 16th century.

Haftarah — weekly Prophetic portion. The selection has some reference to the Biblical portion (Sidrah).

Halachah — Hebrew for "law". Jewish religious law which also encompasses the binding rules of action in all spheres of life.

Hanukkah — Hebrew for "dedication"; a festival observed eight days in wintertime, commemorating the victory of Maccabees over the Syrian and Greek invaders in 165 B.C.E., and the rededication of the Holy Temple. Purim — festival of lots commemorating the rescue of the Jews by Queen Esther from a plot of vizier Haman in the Persian exile.

Havdalah — Hebrew for "differentiation"; ritual denoting the cutoff of the sacred Sabbath from mundane workdays.

Hazzan — cantor or sheliach tzibur (a leader of the congregation); he recites prayers leading the service.

Hevrah kaddishah — "holy brotherhood" in Hebrew and Aramaic. A society devoted to providing ritual burial and offering comfort to the mourning family.

Huppah — wedding canopy under which the wedding ritual is performed, symbolising the newlyweds' future home.

Kaporet — drapery covering a device on which the curtain hangs in the top part of the holy ark, see Parochet. Keter Torah — silver crown, a symbol of wisdom and royal majesty which adorns the Torah.

Kippah — skullcap (yarmulke in Yiddish) worn during prayers, a service, or permanently on the head by observant Jews.

Kohen — priest; a descendant of Aaron, the biblical high priest (pl. Kohanim).

Kosher — ritually suitable and permissible food as instructed by the Torah and Talmud.

Levite — offspring of the Biblical tribe of Levites who helped the Temple priestly tribe Kohanim.

Maariv — evening prayer. Pentateuch — "five-part book" in Greek; Five Books of Moses, see the Torah.

Magen David — "shield of David"; six-pointed star, "hexagram" in Greek, a magic symbol of various ancient cultures, a modern symbol of Jewishness and the State of Israel.

Mahzor — book of prayers for individual festivals.

Mappah — binder; a narrow embroidered band of linen which drapes the scroll of the Law (vimpel in Yiddish).

Me'il — Torah mantle which covers, protects and decorates the Torah scroll.

Menorah — symbolical seven-branched candelabrum at the Temple in Jerusalem; at the synagogue it is an eight-branched Hanukkah candelabrum shaped as the Menorah.

Mezuzah — metal or wooden case containing a quote from the Torah, affixed to the right doorpost of a Jew's home.

Mikveh — ritual bath used before the Sabbath, wedding etc which provides especially spiritual cleaning.

Milah — circumcision carried out on the eighth day after a boy's birth, symbolising his entering into a covenant with God.

Minhah — afternoon prayer.

Minyan — quorum of ten males over the age of thirteen; a number necessary for the performance of a religious service, particularly for the reading of the Torah.

Mishnah — "repetition", "study"; a codified collection of religious-legal literature edited in the early 3rd century C.E. by Patriarch Judah ha-Nasi. The Mishna has 6 orders divided into 63 treatises with 524 chapters.

Nefeleh — miscarriage; a designation of a part of the cemetery lot reserved for burials of babies who died within the first year of life.

Ner tamid — eternal light which hangs at the synagogue in front of the holy ark commemorating the Temple in Jerusalem.

Parochet — synagogal curtain covering the door of the holy ark.

Passover — eight-day springtime holiday, one of the Pilgrim festivals, commemorating the exodus of the Israelites from Egyptian bondage.

Passover Haggadah — book of prayers, blessings, narratives and songs related to the exodus from Egyptian bondage, which is read during the Seder meal at Passover.

Purim — festival of lots commemorating the rescue of the Jews by Queen Esther from a plot of vizier Haman in the Persian exile.

Rabbi — Hebrew for "my master", "my teacher"; a spiritual leader of the community; he rules on problems of religious law and acts as a teacher, spiritual adviser and spokesman for the congregation.

Rimmonim — silver finials placed on top of the rollers of the scrolls of the Law, shaped as pomegranates.

Rosh hashanah — New Year observed on the 1st and 2nd days of Tishri (September — October).

Seder — Hebrew for "order"; ceremonial family feast observed on the first two days of Passover and including symbolical food with unleavened bread — matzot.

Sephardic — mediaeval Hebrew term for "Spanish" or "of Spain"; conventional term used to designate the Jews originating from Spain and Portugal.

Shabbat — Sabbath, the seventh day of the week, Saturday, the most important of Jewish festivals whose observance is required by the 4th commandment.

Shacharit — morning prayer.

Shavuoth — feast of weeks; a two-day festival commemorating the giving of the Law to Moses on Mount Sinai.

Shiviti — tablet with a quote of Psalm 16:8, placed on the hazzan's pulpit or a pulpit for the reading of the Torah.

Siddur — book of prayers for week days, the Sabbath and New month.

Sidrah — weekly portion of the Torah. The Torah is divided into 54 portions which are read every week throughout the year.

Sukkah — booth; a provisional dwelling with an

open roof to observe the Feast of Tabernacles.

Sukkoth — festival of tabernacles observed in the autumn, celebrating the completion of the harvest, and reminding Jews of the 40 years of their ancestors wandered in the wilderness on their way from Egypt. It is observed in provisional tabernacles.

Synagogue — „assembly" in Greek; a designation of Jewish religious congregations and buildings in which they took place.

Tallit — prayer shawl; a longitudinal band of linen with fringes recalling the Torah commandments.

Talmud — "teaching", Oral Law; it consists of the Mishnah and Gemara ("improvement, addition"), interpretation of the Mishnah dating from the 3rd to 5th centuries C.E. The Talmud has 2 editions — the Jerusalem Talmud dating from the 4th century, and the Babylonian Talmud from the 5th century C.E.

Tas — silver shield on the Torah scroll, symbolising a breast shield worn by the High Priest at the Temple in Jerusalem.

Tefillin — phylacteries in Greek; leather cases containing Biblical injunctions, which adult men fix on their left arm and forehead while praying.

Temple — Solomon's Holy Temple in Jerusalem built around the mid-10th century B.C.E.; Biblical sanctuary of the Israelites destroyed by Babylonians in 586 B.C.E. The second Temple was completed in Jerusalem in 516 B.C.E. and destroyed by Romans in 70 C.E.

Torah — Hebrew for "teaching", "guidance", "law". Generally refers to the Five Books of Moses, the basis of Judaism. It is handwritten in accordance with strict rules on a parchment scroll which is attached to wooden rollers.

Yad — silver pointer shaped as a little hand to point at the text of the Torah while reading.

Yeshiva — traditional Talmudic school of higher learning.

Yom Kippur — Day of Atonement, the most solemn festival of the Jewish calendar, observed in fasting and all-day-long prayers on the 10th day of Tishri. Passover — eight-day springtime holiday, one of the Pilgrim festivals, commemorating the exodus of the Israelites from Egyptian bondage.

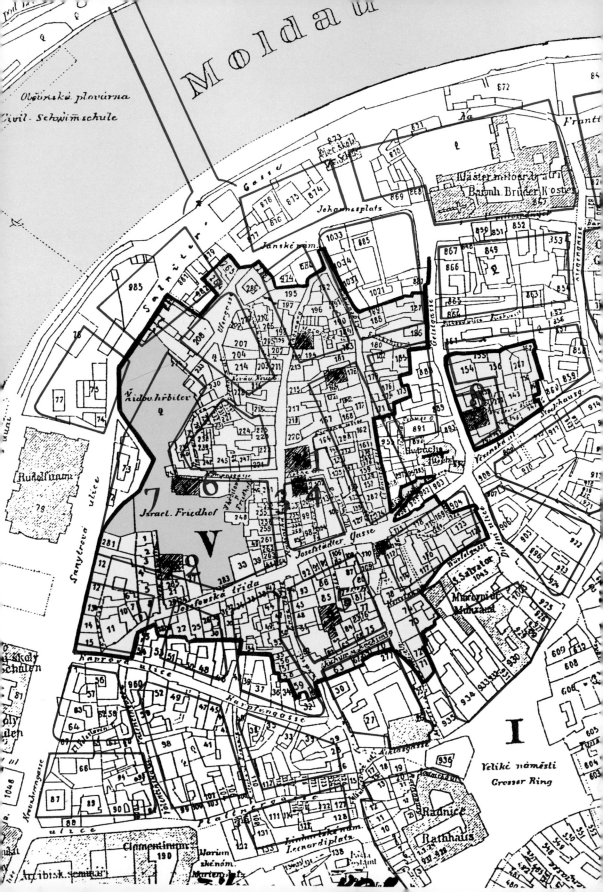